# Beyond the mountain

## True Tales About Montreal

## STUART NULMAN

*Callawind*
Publications Inc.

Beyond the Mountain: True Tales About Montreal

Copyright © 2002 by Stuart Nulman

CATALOGUING IN PUBLICATION DATA
Nulman, Stuart, 1963–
    Beyond the mountain : true tales about Montreal / Stuart Nulman.

Includes bibliographical references and index.
ISBN 1-896511-19-8

    1. Montréal (Quebec)—History. I. Title.

FC2947.4.N84 2002      971.4'28      C2002-903052-8
F1054.5.M857N84 2002

Edited by Christine Marcotte. Indexed by Heather Ebbs.
Designed by Marcy Claman.

10 9 8 7 6 5 4 3 2 1

Printed in Canada.

Callawind Publications Inc.
3539 St. Charles Boulevard, Suite 179, Kirkland, Quebec, Canada H9H 3C4
2083 Hempstead Turnpike, PMB 355, East Meadow, New York, USA 11554-1711
E-mail: info@callawind.com   http://www.callawind.com

# CONTENTS

# aCKNOWLEDGEMENTS

There is an interesting line uttered by Liam Neeson in Steven Spielberg's 1993 Oscar-winning film *Schindler's List*. After he has safely transported and ensconced 1000 Jews from Poland to his factory in Czechoslovakia, Schindler addresses the Nazi soldiers who are assigned to guard the factory, and outlines his strict rules of conduct for them (the main one being that they are not allowed in the factory without his special authorization). After his speech, Schindler grins and tells them rather cheerfully: "For your co-operation, you have my gratitude."

Having the opportunity to write my first book on a subject that is a passion of mine is indeed a dream come true. And if it were not for the co-operation and support of many people, this book would not have been possible. Now is my chance to express my gratitude to them.

» To my publishers Marcy Claman and Lenny Greenfield at Callawind Publications, whom I have known for over 30 years. Had it not been for that fateful encounter at Indigo Books and Music in downtown Montreal in July of 2000, this journey would never had happened, and it's been quite a rewarding journey.

» To my hard-working editor Christine Marcotte, who has managed to meticulously look over every detail of the manuscript and provide invaluable feedback and guidance.

» To Andrew Gryn, Graham MacDonald, Jack Goldsmith, Sharman Yarnell, Joe Morena, Danielle Viger from *La Presse*, the City of Montreal Archives and the McGill University Archives department for supplying the photos and illustrations that grace this book.

» To the Eleanor London Public Library in Côte-Saint-Luc, the Montreal Public Library on Sherbrooke Street East, the Webster and Vanier Libraries at Concordia University, and to Nancy Marelli of Concordia University's Archives department, for allowing me to spend numerous nights and weekends over the course of the last year and a half, digging up all the rich veins of information that form the foundation of this book.

» To my loving and supportive family: my father Norman; my late mother Carol; my sister Nancy; Uncle Barry and Nicole (see, you got your acknowledgement!); in-laws Steven and Lynn; nephews Aidan, Hayes and Gregory; niece Hailey; cousins Allison and Lorne, and Uncle Benny and Auntie Sally Goodman.

» To my brother Andy who for over 15 years has played a vital role in Montreal's cultural history, by running the Just for Laughs comedy festival and building it into the internationally renowned event that it has become, and which has put Montreal on the map. Thank you for the advice, support, and for giving me the chance to get a foot in the book publishing door when I researched your previous two books. Our lives (and libraries) are much richer for it.

» To the people at CBC Montreal, *The Suburban* newspaper, Just for Laughs, CJAD, CAE Inc. (Technical Publications Department) and the kids and staff of the B'nai Brith Youth Organization (in the Laurentian Region Association, Eastern Canada Region, and the international order) for playing a big part in my professional and personal development.

» And to Allan (Fluffy) Schwartz and Eramelinda Boquer, who both truly define what the word "friend" is all about.

Also, this being my first book, I wish my publisher to indulge me and list the following people whom I have encountered during the past 39 years of my life who have offered their encouragement, support and friendship, and although they may not know it, have contributed in their own unique way to the fruition of this book: Irene Aguzzi, Dawn Allen, Robin Altman, David Anber, George Anthony, Wayne Appleby, Julia Asner, Blair Bartrem, Allison Beck, Michael Beigelman, Elliot and Elsa Beker, Rachel Berger, Dr. Laurie Betito, Matt and Deb Beyers, Frank Boivin, Rob Braide, Pat Burke, Mark Burns, Ernie Butler, Jeff Campana, Perry Carmen, Ray Chaisson, George Christy, Lindsey Chrysler, Larry and Elaine Cohen, Mike Cohen, Sheldon Cohen, Matthew Cope, Simon Dardick, David Davis, Annie and Karine Deschamps, Bena, Mark and Tiffany Diamond, Neil Drabkin, Elan Dubrofsky, David Edey, Jeremy Einfrank, Mindy Eklove, Kenny Elman, Lila Feng, Linda Fothergill, Sheldon and Sue Freed, Al Freedman, Richard Friedlander, Cary Friedman, Emma Ganga-Daley, Umberto Garafano, Lynn Garfinkle, Maria Gastaldi, William Gilsdorf, André Gloutnay, Nigel and Daniella Goddard, Mel Goldenberg, Adam Gordon, Al Gravelle, Evan Green, Arnie Greenberg, Marty Greenstein, Jason Guben, E. Jean Guèrin, Ian Halperin, Marc Hamou, Pat Hamou, Linda Henry, Michael and Halley Herman, Bill Hicks,

Bruce and Liz Hills, Suzanne Hinks, Gerry, Miri and Lori Hoch, Jeff Hoffman, Peter Anthony Holder, Frankie Hudak, Neil Janna, Noah Joseph, Leslie, Linda, Jason, Corey, Katie and Ethan Kalman, Lindsay Kantor, Mikey Kaufman, Andy Kindler, Veronica Klein, Elliot Kligman, Shawn Korin, Tania Korin, Steve Lachman, Howard Lapides, Yvon Laplante, Jake Lawrence, Dan Laxer, Sylvie Leblanc, Sylvie Leduc, Leisa Lee, Steven and Amanda Leiva, Mitch and Michal Levi, David Levine, Mark Levine, Carmi Levy, Michael Libling, Jodi Lieberman, Andy Lowenstein, Irwin Margolese, Debbie Marsellos, Craig McPherson, Willie Mercer, Marina Milyavskaya, Rick Moffat, Jason and Elana Muscant, Fred Nicolaidis, John Oakley, Michael O'Brien, Jim Pacheco, Louise Parent, Lise Parizeau, Lorne Perlmutter, Mary Anne Pierro, Jillian Pottel, Linda Quirino, Mark Rennie, Glen Richstone, Danny Robinson, Jeff Rothpan, Steve Rowe, Denis Roy, Gilbert Rozon, Luce and Lucie Rozon, Tim Sarkes, Brent Schiess, George Schlatter, Elana Schneiderman, Steve Schneiderman, Tommy Schnurmacher, Lowell Schreider, Glenn Schwartz, Debra Segal, Scott Sellers, Mark Shainblum, Diane Shatz, Tara Silver, Jack, Barbara, Jeff and Greg Singer, Bobby Slayton, Frank and Frances Smiley, Ezra Soiferman, Jennifer Solomon, Johanna Somers, Claude St. Martin, George Toufexis, George Tucci, David Turoff, Yvon Vadnais, Hélène Vallée, Caroline Van Vlaardingen, Blake Walker, Max Wallace, Oren Weintraub, Lillian Wiseman, Joe Wittenstein, Kathy Wolfe, Michael Wollock, Steven Wollock, Gordie and Judy Zelman. I thank you all very much.

# INTRODUCTION

**M**y interest in Montreal's colourful history can be traced back to May of 1977. *The Montreal Gazette* launched its bicentennial celebrations (which would culminate on June 3 of the following year) by using its vast archives to take a look back in time. For the next two and a half months, *The Gazette*, in its Monday and Wednesday editions, published a reproduction of its front pages from the past and showed how the paper had covered some of the most newsworthy events of the past 200 years, such as the Apollo 11 moon landings, the abdication of King Edward VIII, and the Battle of Waterloo.

However, it was one of their first front-page reproductions that sparked my interest. It was the December 8, 1941 edition, which dealt with the Japanese attack on Pearl Harbor. However, it wasn't the actual front page that caught my attention, but rather the second page, which showed a collection of news items and advertisements from that period. This particular page displayed ads from several Montreal movie theatres that were still standing in 1977, where I saw my fair share of movies as a kid, such as the Palace, the Loews (which showed Greta Garbo's last movie *Two-Faced Woman*), the York, and the Snowdon. There were also four ads for then-popular Montreal nightspots such as the El Morocco and the Esquire Showbar. My father caught a glimpse of these ads and shared with me many of his memories of frequenting those clubs during his late teens and early 20s. He also listed a few of the entertainers that he had seen perform on numerous occasions: Oscar Peterson, Sammy Davis, Jr. and his favourite, Frank Sinatra.

I listened to these stories with rapt attention, and although I was an avid history buff at the time (but leaning more toward British and American history), my curiosity about Montreal's past began to be piqued. That same year, I saw a telecast of Donald Brittain's excellent documentary about the life and times of former mayor Camillien Houde *His Majesty, Mr. Montreal* on CBC Television, which brought to life some of the stories that my dad had told me of the open city that Montreal was during the 1940s and early 1950s. From that point on, Montreal's history became a passion of mine.

Over the next 25 years, I would absorb any book, magazine, news-paper article, television show, documentary, and microfilm that I could get my hands on — in both English and French — to find out more about older Montreal. There was a time about 10 years ago when Montrealers took their history for granted. We were bombarded with labels that were imposed upon the city by the media as being "The Bank Robbery Capitol of Canada", "The Stolen Car Capitol of Canada" and "The Poverty Capitol of Canada".

Montreal has quite a rich history. The only problem is that not many people are aware of it. When we were introduced to it during Canadian history class in high school, it was usually restricted to Jacques Cartier's landing here in 1535, de Maisonneuve and the founding of Ville-Marie in 1642, the capitulation to the British in 1760, and the burning of the Parliament buildings in 1849. There are plenty of interesting facts and stories that just fell through the cracks and have remained buried, rarely to be uncovered. Many people don't know that since its founding 360 years ago, Montreal has had the distinction of being the birthplace of radio in North America and television in Canada, that it was the haven for a presidential assassin, that it was where one of the best-known songs of the 1960s was written and recorded, and that it was where baseball's colour barrier was finally broken . . . and don't forget, that it was the place where bagels and smoked meat were made famous.

However, over the last few years, there has been a wave of articles, books, museum exhibitions and heritage walking tours that have opened the door to a new appreciation of Montreal's past. This is where *Beyond the Mountain* comes in. Why was such a title chosen for this book? According to an article in the April 20, 2002 edition of *The Gazette*, "most people agree that Mount Royal possesses rich symbolic, natural, and cultural values. It is a fundamental part of Montreal's identity." I quite agree. Mount Royal is probably the most recognized part of Montreal's landscape and is the nucleus of what Montreal is all about to both residents and visitors from abroad. But there is so much more to Montreal than the mountain, and this book goes beyond the boundaries to show a lesser known, yet a fascinating side of Montreal's history.

So forget the bank robbery, stolen car and poverty labels associated with Montreal in the past. I prefer "City of Champions", "City of Festivals", "The Cannes of Comedy" and "The Paris of North America". It's more fun that way.

— Stuart Nulman, Montreal, April 2002

# fROM THE FOOTLIGHTS
## OF ST-CATHERINE STREET

### the montreal entertainment scene

**In September of 1964, the Beatles performed their first and only concert in Montreal. Which Beatle was accompanied onstage by a bodyguard because he was receiving death threats?**

➯**Ringo Starr.** When the Fab Four arrived in Montreal on the morning of September 8, they learned from local papers that death threats were being made against Ringo. "Some people decided to make an example of me as an English Jew," recounted Ringo in *The Beatles Anthology*. "The one major fault is, I'm not Jewish."

Although the Beatles usually took such threats in stride, it was the first time that Ringo felt genuinely worried. John, in his usual outspoken fashion, responded to the threats by saying: "We'll not be anybody's pawns. We're here to play music." But as an added measure of security during the show, Ringo put his drum cymbals further up, shielding him slightly from the audience, and crouched lower than usual behind his drum set. "No one was seeing much of me that day," recalled Ringo. Also, a plainclothes policeman sat near him, partially hidden behind the drum riser.

"I started to get hysterical," said Ringo. "I thought — if someone in the audience has a pop at me, what is this guy going to do? Is he going to catch the bullet?"

These threats came in the midst of Beatlemania, a phenomenon that infected thousands of Montreal teens that year. The hysteria began upon their arrival at the Dorval Airport on the morning of the concert. Here, the Beatles were greeted by 5,000 rain-drenched fans hoping for nothing more than a two-minute glimpse of the Fab Four. In total, 117 Royal Canadian Mounted Police officers were on-site to control the crowd.

The Beatles performed two sold-out shows at the Montreal Forum that day, one at 4 p.m. and one at 8:30 p.m. Opening acts included the Righteous Brothers, the Exciters, Jackie DeShannon, and the Bill Black Combo.

 uring the Beatles' 1964 North American tour (where they made stops in Vancouver, Toronto, and Montreal), their repertoire consisted of the following 12 songs (in order of appearance): "Twist and Shout", "You Can't Do That", "All My Loving", "She Loves You", "Things We Said Today", "Roll Over Beethoven", "Can't Buy Me Love", "If I Fell", "I Want To Hold Your Hand", "Boys", "A Hard Day's Night", and "Long Tall Sally". Tickets for the two Beatles shows at the Forum could be purchased for $4.50 and $5.50.

Interestingly, journalists learned in a press conference that, prior to their arrival in Montreal, the Beatles had unanimously decided not to speak any French. However, they changed their tactic more than one year later when a French verse crept into their 1965 hit single "Michelle". Here, the following is sung: "Michelle, ma belle, sont les mots qui vont très bien ensemble, très bien ensemble."

Eight hours after their arrival, the Beatles boarded a plane for Jacksonville, Florida, leaving behind 12 girls needing treatment for hysteria, cuts and bruises, 500 rain-soaked Montreal policemen, one police officer recuperating from a bitten thumb, and 22,000 satisfied fans.

Nothing ever came of the death threats to Ringo Starr, who called the two-show gig at the Forum "the worst gig of my life."

Television came to Canada on September 6, 1952, when Montreal's CBFT Channel 2 went to air. What did CBFT do during its first two years of operation that differed from the years to follow?

→ It operated as a bilingual station. When it made its debut, Montreal and Canada's first television station promoted linguistic harmony by broadcasting an even number of French and English language programs, such as French and English children's films. The first day of airing featured variety programs, a live drama, and a newsreel of the summer's top news events.

Who were some of the first people to speak on television? This honour was bestowed to Prime Minister Louis St. Laurent, CBC chairman

Davidson Dunton, and Dr. Thomas T. Goldsmith, president of the Dumont Corporation, a corporation which, at the time, had a dual role as broadcaster and television set manufacturer.

When CBFT first went on the air on September 6, 1952, television sets were available in 17- or 20-inch models. Prices ranged from $250 to $600.

On an experimental basis, CBFT had been airing programs since June 25 of that year from their studios on Dorchester Boulevard West (now Boulevard René-Lévesque). This programming included sports events (such as a Montreal Royals baseball game from Delorimier Stadium), a live drama presentation, and films.

In its early days, CBFT showed 35 hours of programming each week in both French and English, including the children's puppet show *Pépinot et Capucine, Music Hall, The Big Revue, Uncle Chichimus,* the popular drama series *La Famille Plouffe,* which was presented in both languages (and at one point, had 81 percent of all television sets in Montreal tuned in) and of course, *Hockey Night in Canada/La Soirée du Hockey.*

Less than two years later, on January 10, 1954, Montreal also became the first city in Canada to have two television channels when CBMT, the city's first English television station, made its debut. The Dumont Corporation, keeping in mind its television set manufacturing division, welcomed CBMT in its own unique way in an advertisement that appeared in *The Montreal Star* on January 9, 1954. "There'll be more to see and enjoy as CBMT, Montreal's second TV station begins telecasting, bringing a wider choice of entertainment for every taste. Now, more than ever, you should own a Dumont Teleset."

Its inaugural telecast was *The Small Fry Forum,* a children's panel show that featured, as its first guest, Montreal Canadiens star Elmer Lach, who was peppered with a variety of hockey-related questions from enthusiastic young panellists.

And what about the future of television in Canada? Journalist Gerald Clark told viewers in an article in *Weekend Picture Magazine* on the day that CBFT went to air: "Don't worry about color. Black and white television will be around for years."

**Montreal's first private TV station, CFCF 12, went to air for the first time at 5:45 p.m. on January 20, 1961. What was CFCF 12's debut program?**

➥ *Carte Blanche.* Billed as a "relaxed, sophisticated program of news, views, interviews and weather," *Carte Blanche* was hosted by Jimmy Tapp (who made his name in the 1950s on CBC Television with his popular celebrity interview show *The Tapp Room*), along with news-caster Art Leonard, sports director Brian MacFarlane, and weather person Marj Anthony. During the show's opening, the group shed their journalistic facades and performed a lip-synched production number to the Four Lads' hit song "Another Opening, Another Show".

It was at its temporary studios located at the old Avon Theatre on Laurier Street and Park Avenue (its Ogilvy Avenue facilities would not open until May of that year) that CFCF 12 launched *Carte Blanche.* After three weeks of dry runs on closed-circuit television (in which Jimmy Tapp admitted that he interviewed a coat rack and commented that it was "a great bit of dialogue"), producer Jerry Rochon promised potential viewers that CFCF 12's flagship show would feature "people in the headlines, informed opinions on everything from decorating to diet, discussions by authoritative speakers on local news, interviews with how-to experts, razor-sharp news reports and reviews, featurettes, weather, and the latest in sports and sports interviews."

Carte Blanche *host Jimmy Tapp (left) interviewing a young comedian named Jackie Mason* (circa 1961).

Its first broadcast was a packed one, lasting a total of 75 minutes. An interview with mayor Jean Drapeau was followed by an introduction of CFCF 12's cast of on-air personalities and a presentation of what the new station would offer its viewers, notably a wide variety of local and American programming.

The remainder of CFCF 12's opening day included the panel discussion show *Project One, Sunset Theatre,* an early evening movie showcase hosted by Jack Curran, which screened the 1949 production of *A Connecticut Yankee in King Arthur's Court* with Bing Crosby, *The Andy Griffith Show, Lock-Up* with Macdonald Carey, the first broadcast of the station's long-running newscast *Pulse,* and concluded at 11 p.m. with *Pajama Playhouse,* a late-night movie program hosted by breathless-sounding, lingerie-wearing Pajama Patty, who welcomed night owl viewers into her living room with a presentation of Cecil B. deMille's 1947 historical drama *Unconquered,* starring Gary Cooper.

A pioneer in radio (in 1919, it was the first radio station in North America to go on-air), CFCF applied for a television station licence as early as 1938, during radio's golden age, but did not succeed in obtaining it until March of 1960.

Owned and operated by the Canadian Marconi Company, CFCF 12 hoped to capture Montreal's cosmopolitan flavour by offering its viewers five locally produced live shows including *Carte Blanche, Pajama Playhouse, Sunset Theatre* and *Surprise Party,* a 45-minute kids' program starring (Magic) Tom Auburn, and by broadcasting 12 US-imported programs such as *77 Sunset Strip, Route 66, The Real McCoys* and *Playboy's Penthouse.*

**What popular 1960s anthem was recorded by John Lennon and Yoko Ono in Room 1742 of the Queen Elizabeth Hotel on June 1, 1969?**

→ **"Give Peace a Chance".** It was recorded during their second bed-in for peace (their first was at the Amsterdam Hilton in March of that year). John and Yoko originally wanted to hold the event in New York City but US authorities refused to grant Lennon a visa because of his November 1968 drug conviction. Montreal was the next best choice because of its close proximity to the US border and because their message of peace could easily be relayed to the States via this town.

During their week at the Queen Elizabeth Hotel, John and Yoko welcomed as many visitors as possible, including radio and television broadcasters, journalists (among them cartoonist and *Lil' Abner* creator Al Capp) and, with the help of a few co-operative Montreal disc jockeys, connected to several randomly selected American disc jockeys, asking them to spread their message of peace. CJAD broadcaster and Gazette columnist Tommy Schnurmacher was also present at the bed-in. A 19-year-old McGill University student at the time, Schnurmacher volunteered to babysit Yoko's daughter Kyoko (from her first husband Tony Cox, a British film director) and took her for walks at a nearby park.

On June 1, Lennon, with a few friends and visitors (such as Tommy Smothers and Timothy Leary), crowded into Room 1742 and recorded "Give Peace a Chance" in five minutes flat. Taped on borrowed professional equipment and with Lennon on acoustic guitar and lead vocals, "Give Peace a Chance" was released in the United Kingdom on July 4, 1969, and although it is credited to the Plastic Ono Band, was the first solo single released by a Beatles member.

"Give Peace a Chance" continues to be regarded today as one of the world's most established peace anthems and slogans.

**The showbiz marriage of the 1960s was held in Montreal at the prominent Ritz-Carlton Hotel on March 15, 1964. Which stars exchanged vows that day?**

➥**Richard Burton and Elizabeth Taylor.** The couple, who met while filming the epic film *Cleopatra* two years earlier, were married at 2:30 p.m. at the Royal Suite (Room 810) of the Ritz. The small, low-key, single-ring ceremony was presided by Rev. Leonard Mason of the Unitarian Church and was attended by 11 people, mainly employees of either Burton or Taylor (Bob Wilson, Burton's valet, served as best man). As a wedding gown, Taylor wore a replica of the yellow gown that she had been wearing when filming her first *Cleopatra* scene with Burton.

The wedding was originally scheduled to take place in Toronto, where Burton was appearing in a production of *Hamlet* with Sir John Gielgud. However, the Ontario government would not grant the couple a marriage licence, mainly because they did not recognize the validity of Taylor's Mexican divorce from her previous husband, singer Eddie Fisher, finalized only 10 days before. It was Montreal lawyer Max Bernfeld who arranged to have the marriage take place in Montreal.

After the ceremony, Burton released a statement to the press saying: "Elizabeth and I are very happy." But this terse sentence did not reveal his actual mood before the wedding. In fact, he was in a foul mood from the moment they took off from Toronto on the morning of the wedding. By the time the ceremony was about to take place, Burton was drunk and growing impatient with the fact that Taylor was 45 minutes late, which prompted him to blurt out "Isn't that fat little tart here yet? I swear to you she'll be late for the last bloody judgment!"

To ensure the newlywed's privacy, uniformed policemen were stationed on the eighth floor of the Ritz, making the floor virtually impenetrable to outsiders, especially reporters. One exception was Gazette reporter David Tafler, who managed to slip through security and make his way to Taylor and Burton's suite. He knocked on the door of Room 810 and was greeted by a grumpy, confused Burton dressed in a bathrobe, who slammed the door in his face.

**What landmark 1957 McGill-produced musical revue, which satirized Canadian culture and identity, became a smash hit not only in Montreal but also in the rest of Canada?**

➥ *My Fur Lady.* Featured as McGill University's main attraction, and put on by the 1957 Red and White Revue, *My Fur Lady* was a musical revue that satirized anything and everything Canadian, from politics to education, social mores, and the quest for a distinctive Canadian flag. The success of *My Fur Lady,* and how it proved that Canadians could poke fun and laugh at themselves, influenced future Canadian satirical sketch comedy shows such as *The Royal Canadian Air Farce* and *This Hour Has 22 Minutes.*

Written by McGill students Timothy Porteus, Donald MacSween and Eric Wang, the show's premise was centred in Mukluko, an Eskimo territory north of Canada. The Muklukoans had as their mission to get their princess married before she came of age (which was in one month's time) or else, get annexed to Canada. The princess was sent to Ottawa to find a husband. Instead, she found the Governor General, who was only interested in culture, and a newspaper reporter who taught her about Canada through songs and sketches.

*Before* Air Farce *and* This Hour has 22 Minutes, *there was* My Fur Lady, *McGill's groundbreaking satirical revue (1957).*

But why put together a topical, made in Canada student revue that satirized the Canadian identity? In a newspaper interview, Porteus explained that it was the right time for such a production. "No one who has lived in Canada for the past few years can be unaware of our changing attitude towards existence as a distinct national entity. No university student who has been aware of the change, and proud of it, can resist the temptation to poke some fun at its more extreme manifestations." He added that *My Fur Lady* gave him and the members of the Red and White Revue the obligation and opportunity to cast a disrespectful eye on the doings of Canada's elders and contemporaries.

What was the most difficult part of writing the play? According to Porteus, it was writing songs that parodied great Canadian women of the day and Canadian culture. "Not enough," he lamented.

*My Fur Lady* opened on February 7, 1957, at McGill's Moyse Hall and was slated for a six-day run. However, word of mouth about this sharp, biting satire was overwhelmingly positive. Hundreds of people applied for tickets and many more were turned away at the door each night. The run was extended to 14 days.

The critics were just as enthusiastic. Montreal Star theatre critic Sydney Johnson proclaimed *My Fur Lady* as the best-produced Red and White Revue in 10 years. He said: "[*My Fur Lady* is a] thoroughly Canadian revue that could not have been produced in any other than a Canadian institution and could only be appreciated to the full by a Canadian audience." *My Fur Lady* later embarked on an equally successful Canadian tour.

**Something peculiar happened during the Place des Arts' gala opening on September 22, 1963. What was it?**

➥**A demonstration and riot by a group of Quebec separatists took place.** Two Quebec separatist groups, the Rassemblement pour L'Indépendence Nationale (RIN) and the Parti Republicain du Québec, demonstrated to protest how Place des Arts' finances were run. They did not agree with the appointment of an American as its administrative director and were sympathetic to the Montreal Union des Artistes' dispute over affiliation issues with Place des Arts performers.

The protest started outside the hall on the corner of St-Catherine and Jeanne-Mance streets at 8:30 p.m., at the same time as the opening gala was scheduled to begin. After 200 demonstrators heard speeches by the leaders of the two participating groups, a mob of youths clad in leather jackets began inciting protesters. Mounted policemen contained the mob to a parking lot near the hall but things gradually worsened. While shouting slogans such as "Québec Libre!", "FLQ", and "Place des Arts — Place of Pigs", the angry group pelted policemen with rocks, jeered some of the fancy dressed gala guests, blocked traffic, and damaged parked cars.

**D**uring the opening night gala at the Grande Salle of Place des Arts, a framed reprint of an article that appeared in *The Canadian Spectator* in 1878 was on display in the lower level of the lobby. The headline read: "Montreal must have a concert hall."

Nineteen rioters were arrested and charged with a variety of offences including assaulting a police officer, possessing an offensive weapon (a duelling rapier sword), and disturbing the peace.

The general public reacted with disgust to this demonstration. One Quebec City businessman said: "These people are giving all French-Canadians a bad name . . . if they have a grievance, let them take it to the authorities with dignity."

For the most part, the 3,000 guests attending the Montreal Symphony Orchestra event that night were not deterred by the demonstration. In fact, many arrived an hour early and were not even aware it had taken place.

Among those participating in the opening gala were Louis A. Lapointe, president of the Sir George-Étienne Cartier Corporation (the administrative body that ran Place des Arts) and Sir Wilfrid Pelletier, founder of the Montreal Symphony Orchestra.

**Frank Sinatra performed his first solo concert in Montreal on November 24, 1944, but was harshly denounced by a Westmount Anglican priest. Why?**

➥**Because his show took place on a Sunday.** In an item in *The Montreal Daily Star,* Anglican priest Rev. Canon G. Oliver of the St. Matthias Church in Westmount denounced the popular singer not for whipping up his young fans into a frenzy, or for his songs, but rather, for the fact that his show was taking place on a Sunday.

During his sermon that day, Rev. Oliver urged his parishioners to protest the fact that the Sabbath was being abused, labelling anyone who attended the Sinatra show as "morons" and deeming the promoters as "pandering to the emotions of the emotionally immature".

"Are we never to make [sic] a stand? Surely the vested interests have time during six days of the week to make money with [sic] encroaching of the Christian Sunday," preached the bombastic minister.

But the pontificating of Rev. Oliver did not stop Sinatra or the 10,000 fans in attendance. The lights dimmed at 9 p.m. and the show began with a 30-minute opening act by Montreal bandleader Allan McIver and his 50-piece orchestra, followed by Sinatra who performed such hits as "Lullaby", "Old Man River", and "Night and Day".

Sinatra earned a princely $10,000 for his performance and a rather highbrow judgment, not from another clergyman, but from critic Roy Kerwin of *The Montreal Daily Star,* who admired Sinatra's vocal phrasing but attributed his enormous success as a singer to his youth and not his talent. "Even the untrained unevenness of his voice contributes to that aura of callow youth which gives him so much in common with his more numerous admirers. The voice itself is not objectionable," he said.

No matter the reason, additional seats had to be added to the Forum to handle the increased demand for tickets.

The 29-year-old Sinatra seemed rather unaware of, if not indifferent, to the criticism.

**A full-scale riot occurred during the Rolling Stones' concert at the Forum on July 17, 1972. What was the cause of this riot?**

➥**Counterfeit tickets.** Chanting "Let us in! Let us in," 500 fans, disappointed that they had been sold counterfeit tickets, soon became unruly. Minor scuffles broke out and after 10 minutes, the 1,000-strong police force stationed outside the Forum changed into riot gear.

The crowd grew uglier. Bottles were thrown at a bus filled with 50 policemen and a powdery substance was tossed at the mobile units of CFCF Radio and CKAC, causing them to burst into flames. A total of 13 people were arrested, including three individuals for peddling the forged tickets that served as the main cause of the riot.

The ticket riot was not the only thing that made the Stones' Montreal leg of their 1972 tour a nightmarish experience. The night before the show, two sticks of dynamite exploded underneath one of their equipment vans parked outside the Forum. A total of 30 speaker cones were destroyed. Although new ones were rushed by jet from the group's equipment supplier in Los Angeles (and made it to Montreal only two hours before showtime), the experience deeply upset lead singer Mick Jagger. "I don't want to go on tonight," he told a reporter from *Weekend, The Montreal Star's* Saturday colour magazine supplement.

*Mick Jagger rocks a packed, sweltering Montreal Forum during the Rolling Stones' 1972 tour. However, according to* The Montreal Star, *500 fans never got to see the show, as they were sold forged tickets.*

The concert itself was a literal hotbed of rock'n'roll. Over 19,000 fans sweltered inside the Forum where the temperature exceeded 100 degrees. The crowd welcomed Stevie Wonder, the opening act, and then the atmosphere became electric as Jagger, clad in a tight white satiny jumpsuit, jean jacket and denim jockey cap, came onstage.

Promoter Donald Tarlton (a.k.a. Donald K. Donald) comments on the incident of Mick Jagger getting hit by a thrown bottle: "I don't think it was meant to hurt him, probably just someone who was a little juiced and thought Mick would like a drink."

Jagger was rattled by the fans, the shouting and the sporadic firecrackers. To make matters worse, he was accidentally struck in the shin by a bottle lobbed from the audience. He proceeded to sing a weak rendition of "Midnight Rambler" and ended the concert sooner than expected.

The fans left the Forum saying it was a great show; Jagger felt otherwise. Looking tired and washed out at a post-concert party in his hotel room, he told someone: "Not good man. It wasn't good." Montreal Star rock critic Juan Rodriguez agreed with Jagger. "The Stones weren't that hot. They were everything everyone's ever said they were, but they weren't that hot."

It would be another 17 years before the Rolling Stones performed in Montreal again.

**What Chicago-born comedian was best known as the rubber-faced, beanie-wearing, zany children's television host Johnny Jellybean, who entertained a generation of Montreal children on CFCF's *Lunchtime Little Theatre* from 1962 to 1967?**

→**Ted Ziegler.** A graduate of Chicago's prestigious Art Institute, Ziegler made his television debut in 1941 at the age of 14, when he appeared as Scrooge in an experimental production of *A Christmas Carol* for a Chicago television station. He also entertained children in tea rooms and department stores across Chicago, whether it be dressed as a clown, the Easter bunny or Santa Claus.

In 1959, Ziegler joined the Australian television network HSV-7, where he worked as a producer, director and writer. He also appeared in front of the cameras as an emcee for a three-week replacement show, which became so popular that it stretched to a 48-week run.

On the afternoon of September 12, 1962, Ziegler first appeared as the character that he would forever be associated with — Johnny Jellybean. Wearing a candy striped jacket, oversized polka-dot bow tie and jellybean-topped beanie, Ziegler helmed *Lunchtime Little Theatre* on CFCF-TV 12, a 60-minute cavalcade of zaniness, sketches, mock commercials and Little Rascals shorts. It also featured Ziegler's wide array of madcap characters that were just as popular as his Johnny Jellybean persona, such as the Ol' Wrangler, Uncle Schnitzel, Hemlock Bones, Polo the Clown and Enzio Pesta (a takeoff of Italian tenor Ezio Pinza, who starred in the original Broadway production of *South Pacific*). Perhaps the most popular feature of *Lunchtime Little Theatre* was the Squawkbox, a cardboard box suspended from the ceiling, in which Johnny would encourage his studio audience (consisting mainly of screaming enthusiastic kids) to decide what size sledgehammer he should use to hit the box: the Masher, Basher or the Smasher (the obvious choice was the much larger Smasher).

The character of Johnny Jellybean did not originate with Ted Ziegler in Montreal. It began in New York City in December of 1956. Bill Britten, a veteran nightclub performer, puppeteer, and circus clown, became the first Johnny Jellybean on *Time For Fun*, a kids' show on Channel 7 in New York. When Britten left the show in August of 1958, he was succeeded by Keith Hefner (brother of *Playboy* magazine founder Hugh Hefner), who donned the jellybean beanie until *Time For Fun* went off the air in 1960. Ziegler became the third and final incarnation of Johnny Jellybean two years later.

The show was very popular, with an average of 190,000 Montreal households tuned in between 12 noon and 1 p.m. Ziegler enjoyed his job as a children's television show host and relished every opportunity to work his wild sense of humour with his young admirers. "They're entertaining and unpredictable, and they love to be entertained," said Ziegler in a 1968 interview with *The Montreal Star*. As well, Ziegler, who earned a degree in educational psychology from Ohio Wesleyan College, was a credited child psychologist and worked part-time for the Protestant School Board of Greater Montreal, using his Johnny Jellybean character to help problem and abused children open up and talk about their situations.

In the fall of 1967, Ziegler ended *Lunchtime Little Theatre* after five years on CFCF and replaced it with a morning children's sitcom called *The Buddies,* in which he starred with Montreal comedian Peter Cullen. The show dealt with the misadventures of commander Bi Bi Latuque (Cullen) and his hapless assistant space cadet Wilbur (Ziegler), both of whom worked on an isolated refuelling station in outer space while causing all sorts of trouble. *The Buddies* ran for one season on CFCF.

During the late 1960s, Ziegler kept a high profile in the Montreal entertainment scene, making numerous personal appearances as Johnny Jellybean at restaurants, birthday parties and shopping centres, and appeared in several ensemble comedy revues such as *Funny You Should Say That* on CBC Radio.

In the early 1970s, Ziegler left Montreal for Los Angeles and, along with Peter Cullen, became a writer and regular cast member of *The Sonny and Cher Comedy Hour* on CBS, which ran from 1971 to 1974. He also made numerous appearances on television shows such as *M\*A\*S\*H.*

Ted Ziegler, wearing his old Johnny Jellybean striped jacket, made his final appearance in Montreal in November of 1992, on the CFCF interview program *Montreal AM Live* to celebrate the 30th anniversary of *Lunchtime Little Theatre's* debut. He died on December 15, 1999 at the age of 72. The following week, as a tribute to him, CFCF ran a farewell piece that contained a rare promotional clip for *Lunchtime Little Theatre* which was filmed in a Montreal candy factory that manufactured — what else — jellybeans.

*Ted Ziegler (second from left) and fellow CFCF children's television host (Magic) Tom Auburn (right) pictured with two young admirers (1982).*

# tHE DARK SIDE
## OF THE CITY

### montreal's notorious crimes, disasters and scandals

In the spring of 1963, Montreal was rocked by a series of bombings by the radical separatist group the Front de Libération du Québec (FLQ). During a rash of mailbox bombings in the predominantly English-speaking suburb of Westmount on May 17, what happened to Canadian Forces officer Sergeant Major Walter Leja?

➡He was seriously injured when a bomb exploded in his hands.

The bombing campaign began in earnest on April 19 when the FLQ planted a bomb behind the Royal Canadian Mounted Police's headquarters in Westmount, which the FLQ labelled as a "colonial stronghold". The following evening, another bomb exploded near the Canadian Army's recruiting centre on Sherbrooke Street West, which killed Wilfred O'Neil, a 65-year-old night watchman.

The FLQ's motive was to achieve Quebec independence through violent means. According to an FLQ communiqué released in March of 1963 following the bombings of three Canadian Army barracks in Montreal, they fought "against Anglo-Saxon colonialism and its flunkies of Quebec bourgeoisie." More particularly, they targeted federal institutions, all information media that held them in contempt, businesses and commercial establishments that did not operate in French, and factories that discriminated and exploited French-speaking employees.

On May 17, the FLQ's bombing campaign worsened. At 3 a.m., a bomb planted in a Westmount mailbox exploded and woke residents of the elite neighbourhood. Within 20 minutes, four more mailbox bombs exploded. Police and post office officials began to inspect mailboxes in the area.

When bombs were found, the Quebec command of the Canadian Army was asked to intervene.

Sergeant Major Walter Leja of the Royal Canadian Engineers, a 42-year-old quartermaster and clerk at the Westmount Armoury, volunteered to defuse the mailbox bombs. Although he had knowledge of explosives, Leja was not a bomb disposal expert. Accompanied by Lieutenant Douglas Simpson, Leja effortlessly dismantled two mailbox bombs in less than 30 minutes.

By the time he arrived at the scene of the third bomb, Leja was joined by Montreal Star photographer Adrian Lunny and was being watched by a group of spectators standing 200 feet away. Leja opened the mailbox and discovered that the bomb was like the other two that he had dismantled (made up of four sticks of dynamite attached to a ticking mechanism). "I'll dismantle this one, too. I have ample time according to the timing mechanism," he said. But as Leja was removing the bomb from the mailbox, it blew up in his hands.

Lunny, who was 10 feet away from Leja, said the explosion sounded like "a 20-pounder cannon being fired". Describing the scene, he said: "He (Leja) just crumpled . . . The mailbox disintegrated. Metal chunks flew in all directions. A piece of metal the size of a typewriter flew over my head . . . Sergeant Major Leja fell sideways and lay in a heap on the sidewalk. He was covered in blood. He didn't move at all. We all rushed toward him. The police were the first to get to him. They brought in first aid and oxygen . . . At first they thought he was dead. But then they saw him breathing and one of the police officers clapped an oxygen mask over his face. The sergeant major didn't move or make a sound."

Leja was rushed to St. Mary's Hospital where he underwent a five-hour operation. He suffered severe injuries to his face and chest and his left arm was amputated. As a consequence of the explosion, he suffered brain damage, was confined to a wheelchair, had weak eyesight, and wore an artificial left arm.

Twenty-one years later, when *The Gazette* caught up with him at St. Anne's Hospital for Veterans in the western Montreal suburb of Sainte-Anne-de-Bellevue, Leja expressed his dissatisfaction at the fact that Jean-Denis Lamoreaux, the FLQ terrorist who had planted the mailbox bomb that seriously injured him, served only 33 months in jail for his crime and was recently appointed communications director for Quebec Premier René Lévesque.

In total, 10 bombs were planted in Westmount on May 17, of which six exploded (including the one that seriously injured Leja, who was that day's only casualty).

**The Caron Commission released its controversial report on October 8, 1954. This report caused shock waves among the Montreal Police Department. What was the subject of the Caron Commission?**

→**Corruption in Montreal and in particular, corruption in the Montreal Police Department.**

From September 1950 to April 1953, the Commission of Inquiry into Gambling and Commercialized Vice in Montreal, presided by Quebec Superior Court Justice François Caron, studied how top officials in City Hall and the police department, through bribery and other corrupt practices, protected and tolerated the activities of Montreal's organized crime syndicate, especially in the gambling and prostitution rackets.

The commission was created by Pacifique Plante who, during the late 1940s, was the police department's assistant director. Plante, who clashed with Montreal police director Albert Langlois, conducted a series of unannounced raids that resulted in the closure of numerous organized gambling and prostitution operations. This did not sit well with Langlois and Plante was suspended and later dismissed for insubordination.

That same year, a private group of citizens and members of the Montreal Executive Committee attempted to investigate vice conditions in the city but failed. It wasn't until Plante published his own findings about crime and corruption in the newspaper *Le Devoir* that the public realized the level of corruption in their city's administration. A newly formed Civic Action League (CAL) party and various church groups lobbied for an inquiry, which was granted by the Quebec Superior Court.

When the Caron Commission report was released in 1954, it included recommendations of ways to clean up the Montreal Police Department, such as:
» That a checks and balances system for dealing with vice matters be established (which should be handled only by district officers and the morality squad)
» That no modifications to the city's padlock laws be issued
» That no bail be granted without the presence of a judge.

For 31 months, the Caron Commission conducted sittings, heard testimonies, amassed exhibits, and endured long, tedious hours of research. Costing $500,000, it became the costliest and lengthiest vice probe in the history of both Montreal and Canada.

On October 8, 1954, Room 24 of the Old Montreal Court House was packed with hundreds of people awaiting Judge Caron's decision on the findings of his commission.

The judgment was divided into two parts: it was found that tolerance of vice had lasted under the directorship of Langlois and his predecessor, Fernand Dufresne, and the judgment was followed with a detailed history of police corruption. Some of the incidents described included:

» How Dufresne had allowed brothels to operate like businesses without any interference from the police for many years.

» How, under Langlois' term, police had conducted an "apartment system" to deal with the underworld gambling establishments. Operators changed their apartment number each month so that while one was raided and padlocked by the police, they could switch to another apartment and operate their gambling establishment as before with little or no interruptions.

» How one police captain, through his corrupt dealings, had saved up $20,000.

Langlois was fired as police director and was fined $500, and Dufresne was banned from holding any civil office position for 10 years, in addition to being fined $7,000. As well, other current and former members of the police department brass were convicted of corruption, were fired, and were fined up to $7,000 each.

Plante returned to the Montreal Police Department, first as assistant director and then as director, and continued to conduct raids on Montreal's illegal operations with the help of the Royal Canadian Mounted Police. Soon American gambling bosses were driven out of Montreal and the federal revenue department was auditing the books of several local mobsters. Constant visits by police officers to their establishments forced them to relocate to the suburbs.

But the sweeping anti-vice reforms brought about by the Caron Commission did not last long. Langlois appealed the commission's decision and in March of 1956, the Quebec Superior Court overturned his dismissal and the city was ordered to reinstate him as police director with two years of back pay. With the defeat of mayor Drapeau in the 1957 election to Sarto Fournier (who was allegedly backed by the mob), the Montreal underworld's illegal activities and the old-style practice of corrupt politics at City Hall underwent a revival that lasted until Drapeau's re-election in 1960.

## What Jewish Montreal Member of Parliament was arrested and tried as a spy in 1946?

↪**Fred Rose.** Born Fred Rosenberg in Lublin, Poland, in 1907, Rose narrowly won a seat in the Montreal riding of Cartier in 1943, representing the Labor-Progressive Party (the new name given to the Communist Party of Canada). Rose was a passionate crusader against injustice and supported the downtrodden.

However, in 1946, Igor Gouzenko, a cipher clerk at the Soviet Embassy in Ottawa, defected. He proceeded to tell the Royal Canadian Mounted Police that a Communist espionage network was being run at the Soviet Embassy and mentioned that Fred Rose was part of the spy ring. He explained that he was working closely with the NKVD, the Russian secret police, and that he was the spy ring's contact man. "(Rose) was the main cog in the network which was conspiring to stab Canada in the back," said Gouzenko, who supported his accusations with paperwork.

On March 14, 1946, Rose was arrested and charged with conspiracy under the Official Secrets Act. His crime: persuading Communists to pass important military information to the Soviet Embassy. As well, Rose was accused of trying to recruit prominent chemist Raymond Boyer to the party, a man known for developing a new and improved way of manufacturing an explosive substance called RDX. Rose's trial lasted three weeks during which 150 documents were introduced as evidence, 60 witnesses were heard, and which attracted worldwide attention.

Following Rose's guilty verdict, *The Montreal Star* ran an editorial in which its tone lent itself to the rampant anti-Communist paranoia and sentiment of the time. It read: "His fate must offer a salutary lesson to others who share his views and who might, in similar circumstances, be tempted to place the interests of some other country before those of the land to which they owe and have sworn allegiance . . . Today this man, who has been so far honoured as to be made a member of the country's Parliament, stands condemned. Well may Mr. Justice Lazure say: 'Instead of showing deep gratitude to Canada, you have betrayed the land of your adoption.'"

During the trial, Rose's lawyer Joseph Cohen repeatedly raised countless objections to presiding judge Wilfrid Lazure over the admission of the incriminating documents that were produced by Gouzenko, as they did not originate within the jurisdiction of the court. Also, Rose objected to the fact that Gouzenko was free from prosecution due to diplomatic immunity. Lazure overruled all objections.

On June 20, after only 35 minutes of deliberation, the jury found Rose guilty and sentenced him to six years in jail. That same day, he was suspended from the House of Commons and was not allowed to take his seat or cast a vote. When asked by judge Lazure to comment on his guilty verdict, a shaken Rose said in a low voice: "All I have to say [is] that I have never done anything against the interests of Canada and no matter what has been said, I still say I am not guilty of conspiracy."

On August 9, 1951, Rose was released from St. Vincent de Paul Penitentiary for good behaviour. Shortly after returning to his Clark Street home, Rose refused to discuss his case, politics, or even his future plans. He told Montreal Star reporter Bill Bantey: "I will be frank with you, I have no statement to make. All I will say is that I am happy to be reunited with my family. I won't say anything else because I don't want to start any arguments." Rose, who was not deported from Canada after his release (an amendment to the Citizenship Act that called for deportation of aliens who committed acts of conspiracy was passed after Rose's trial), was tired of the constant police surveillance and returned to his native Poland where he died in 1983.

**McGill medical school graduate Thomas Neill Cream has been linked to what legendary 19th century mass murderer?**

↪ **Jack the Ripper.** In the last moments of Dr. Thomas Neill Cream's life on November 15, 1892, as he was about to be hung for the murder of a London prostitute, he performed a sort of act of self-confession when he uttered in front of the group of witnesses: "I am Jack . . ."

Cream was referring to a grisly series of murders committed by an elusive Jack the Ripper four years earlier, but of which Londoners were still terrified. Coincidentally, present at Cream's hanging was Sir Henry Smith, London's new police commissioner, who was a self-proclaimed authority on the Ripper murders. This confession was enough for Smith to add Cream's name to the growing list of Jack the Ripper suspects.

Suspect or not, Cream's past was marked by passion, corruption, and murder. Born in Scotland in 1850, Cream arrived in Canada four years later, began studying medicine at McGill University in 1872, and graduated in 1876 with honours.

Following more studies in England, Cream began working as an abortionist. When the body of a chambermaid was found in his office in 1878, he was arrested for the crime but was never charged with the murder.

Cream took his abortion practice to Chicago where, in 1880, another woman died from mysterious circumstances. Again, Cream was arrested for the murder and again, he evaded conviction.

In 1881, Cream was arrested for the murder of Daniel Stott, the husband of his lover. Traces of the poison strychnine were found in the dead man's stomach and Cream was found guilty of murder and was sentenced to life in prison at the Illinois State Penitentiary in Joliet.

 ince the 1888 Whitechapel London murders, there have been 176 Jack the Ripper suspects, yet none of them were ever charged for the crimes. The best-known suspect was Prince Albert Victor, Duke of Clarence, who was the eldest son of the Prince of Wales (later King Edward VII). It was alleged that the prince went to Whitechapel to murder the prostitutes responsible for giving him syphilis, which was gradually affecting his brain. However, documentation shows that while the Ripper murders were taking place, the prince was out of the country, and could not possibly have been responsible for the crimes. He died from the effects of syphilis in 1892.

He served 10 years for Stott's murder and was released in 1891. He returned to England and established himself in the slums of South London. It was there that Cream continued his murderous ways. He poisoned four more women and would have gotten away with them had it not been for his carelessness. He bragged of the murders to friends and associates and even gave tours of the murder sites to two people. Unknowingly to Cream, one of them was a police sergeant. He was charged, found guilty, and executed on November 15, 1892.

Cream's confession on the gallows created numerous theories among Ripper enthusiasts and sceptics. The most contentious point was the fact that Cream was serving a prison term in Illinois from 1881 to 1891, making it impossible for him to have committed the 1888 crimes in London. However, there have been rumours and allegations that Cream, through bribing prison officials, won himself an early release from the penitentiary.

Many similarities between Cream and the Ripper have had Ripper enthusiasts believing that the two were the same person; Cream and the Ripper were both infatuated with London prostitutes and made it a point to taunt police with letters written after their ghastly crimes were committed. Experts even claimed that the handwriting on the two letters that Jack the Ripper sent to the London police matched that of Cream's.

But the fact that Cream's *modus operandi* for his crimes was poisoning and not mutilation, along with the fact that Cream was serving a 10-year prison term in Illinois at the time when the Ripper murders were being committed, makes Thomas Neill Cream a doubtful Jack the Ripper suspect.

**What southwestern Montreal suburb was the site of a massive gas explosion in March of 1965, in which 27 people were killed, and that destroyed an entire block of apartment dwellings?**

➡**LaSalle.** On the morning of March 1, 1965, at 8 a.m., the municipality of LaSalle was awakened by a loud gas explosion on the corner of Bergevin and Jean Milot streets. The explosion destroyed a three-storey, U-shaped apartment complex and was so powerful, according to many witnesses, that it blew the roof right off the building.

Coincidentally, this was not the first gas explosion in this area. On the morning of August 28, 1956, a gas explosion and fire levelled numerous apartments on Des Oblats Street in LaSalle — just around the block from where the 1965 explosion occurred. The blast, which killed seven people, was allegedly set off when a digging machine called a grader broke a gas pipe. An investigation was inconclusive, saying that it could have also been set off when someone lit a match near the pipe or flicked on a light switch.

Dr. Lionel Boyer, LaSalle's mayor, told *The Montreal Star* that he blamed the Quebec Natural Gas Company. According to him, they should have inspected the gas line and the building's equipment on a monthly basis instead of only annually. All apartments in the building were equipped with gas stoves and gas space heaters.

The LaSalle community and all levels of government were quick to rally together to help. Within minutes of the explosion, firemen, policemen and volunteer civil protection workers were on-site with 400 Royal Canadian Navy sailors, originally in the area for training, but who quickly volunteered to help.

# CITY OF LASALLE

The Mayor, the Council and the Citizens of LaSalle wish to thank wholeheartedly all persons, societies and corporations who responded spontaneously by giving of their help, services, employees, . . . finally, by generous contributions of all kinds, on the occasion of the terrible accident of March 1st, and more particularly, without limitation:—

The Royal Canadian Navy, the Provincial Government, the Health Units, Hospitals, the Clergy, the Medical profession, the Red Cross, the St. John Ambulance, the Civil Protection, Scouts & Guides.

The Municipalities of Brossard, Champlain, Cote St-Luc, Croydon, d'Anjou, Dorval, Greenfield Park, Hampstead, Lachine, Longueuil, Montreal, Montreal-North, Montreal-West, Mount-Royal, Notre-Dame du Sacre Coeur, Pierrefonds, Pointe-Aux-Trembles, Pointe Claire, Roxboro, St-Lambert, St-Laurant, St Pierre, St Therese. Valleyfield, Verdun, Westmount.

The industries, the commercial establishments, the Social Clubs, News Agencies, Radio and T.V. Stations, newspapers, all volunteers, etc. . . .

We are sorry being unable to give the names of all those persons who generously contributed to this humanitarian cause.

We can assure them of our deepest gratitude. Their gesture of human solidarity shall always be remembered.

**DR. LIONEL BOYER,**
Mayor.

*A newspaper advertisement placed by LaSalle mayor Lionel Boyer in appreciation of the widespread aid efforts following the devastating gas explosion of March 1, 1965.*

Four emergency blood donor clinics were set up in downtown Montreal and an appeal for donations of items such as clothing, food and blankets was overwhelmingly successful. The Quebec government, following Premier Jean Lesage's visit to the site of the wreckage the afternoon of the explosion, also allocated $500,000 to the aid of the survivors. On the federal level, Prime Minister Lester B. Pearson and Cardinal Paul Émile Léger, along with Premier Lesage and mayor Boyer, set up the City of LaSalle Disaster Fund to coordinate, collect and distribute all monetary donations. The nearby suburb of Lachine also voted to donate $2,000. A telethon organized by Montreal's entertainment community also collected $132,000 in pledges.

Four days after the explosion, a grateful mayor Boyer, on behalf of the council and citizens of LaSalle, placed an advertisement in the newspaper thanking everyone for their support. "We can assure them of our deepest gratitude. Their gesture of human solidarity shall always be remembered."

On January 9, 1927, a fire at the Laurier Palace Theatre killed 78 people, many of whom were children. This disaster prompted the provincial government to pass a law that prohibited the admission of children under the age of 16 to all movie theatres. What was the ironic title of the movie playing as part of a triple bill that fateful Sunday matinee?

→ *Get 'Em Young,* a comedy starring Stan Laurel (in his pre-Laurel & Hardy days), which was part of a triple bill that featured *Sparrows,* a melodrama about abandoned orphans starring Mary Pickford, and *The Devil's Gultch,* a five-reel western flick produced by R-C Pictures, a film company owned by Joseph P. Kennedy, father of future US President John F. Kennedy.

Sunday January 9, 1927, was a chilly winter day and many juvenile moviegoers were eager to escape the winter cold and gathered at the Laurier Palace Theatre, located on St-Catherine and Desery streets.

It was during the showing of *Get 'Em Young* that one of the young patrons seated in the balcony, 18-year-old Charles Pelletier, noticed flames and smoke coming through one of the cracks of the balcony floor. He cried "Fire! Fire!" and the balcony crowd, mainly composed of children between the ages of 5 and 18, began rushing toward the exits. A theatre employee blocked the doorway and urged the scared children to go back to their seats, telling them that there was no danger.

The tragedy received much media coverage across North America. One of the most memorable was from *La Presse,* who published pictures of most of the young victims, either dressed in their first communion or confirmation outfits, or dead as they lay on the sidewalk outside of the theatre.

But by then, it was too late. The frightened children tried to fight their way down the narrow staircase, but the dense smoke overcame those at the front. A pile of bodies eight deep began forming in the small, tight staircase. Most children became trapped and died of asphyxiation.

The first rescuer to arrive at the scene was police officer Augustin Jolin. Not able to rescue the people trapped in the staircase, and still hearing screams and groans, he cut a hole underneath the stairs and started pulling people out. By the time the fire department arrived, the grim task of pulling dead bodies had begun.

The scene at the city morgue was almost as gruesome. Over 150 mothers and fathers presented themselves to identify the bodies of

A plaque commemorating the tragic fire at the Laurier Palace Theatre in 1927 (now a church).

their children. Parents were let in a few at a time to view the rows of bodies and "agonized wails continually indicated that another victim had been identified," *The Montreal Daily Star* sadly reported.

Some families had the misfortune of losing more than one child in the fire. This was the case for police constable Albert Boisseau. While guarding a number of bodies that lay on the sidewalk, he discovered his three children: two daughters and a son ages 8 to 13. "I have no family now," Constable Boisseau said.

Shock settled among Montrealers and Canadians. Messages of condolences were received from abroad by King George V, the Prime Minister of Australia, and the President of France.

As Montreal buried its 78 little victims, immediate action was taken by city coroner Edward McMahon. As a result, many startling revelations were made public about the theatre and how it was run. The Laurier Palace had no operating licence (it was suspended), and was in violation of several municipal and provincial laws, including allowing minors into the theatre unaccompanied, and overcrowding. Also, it was learned that one month prior, the Laurier Palace had experienced a minor fire in the cellar, yet the box office had continued to sell tickets.

The inquest revealed that all the children died from asphyxiation and were all seated in the theatre's balcony section, where the 10-cent admission price was more affordable than the 25-cent or 35-cent admission in the orchestra section.

Coroner McMahon ruled that a dropped cigarette started the fire.

On March 22, 1928, as a result of the tragic consequences that arose from the Laurier Palace Theatre fire, the Quebec government passed an amendment to the Moving Picture Act which stated that movie theatres across the province were prohibited to "receive, in any way, at such shows, any child less than sixteen years of age, whether accompanied or not." The law remained in effect for 40 years.

**In December of 1962, two Ville St-Laurent policemen were shot and killed while trying to foil a bank robbery on Côte de Liesse Road. One of the largest manhunts in Canadian history ensued. According to witnesses, one of the robbers was disguised as what well-known fictional character?**

➡ **Santa Claus.** On the morning of December 14, 1962, Ville St-Laurent police constables Claude Marineau and Denis Brabant were driving down Côte de Liesse Road, test driving a brand new police ambulance vehicle.

Although not on duty that day, they received a call dispatching them to the Canadian Imperial Bank of Commerce on Côte de Liesse Road where a robbery was taking place. As they pulled into the parking lot, they spotted one of the robbers throwing one of the money filled bags into a white Oldsmobile. The other robber was exiting the bank, armed with a Belgian FN.308 submachine gun, wearing sunglasses, and sporting a Santa Claus suit.

Before Marineau and Brabant had a chance to get out of the vehicle and draw their weapons, the robbers opened fire. Marineau jumped out of the car and began returning fire but was shot in the chest and died instantly. Brabant also got out but was strafed in the thigh with bullets from the Santa Claus robber. The robber continued firing and, as Brabant lay dying, approached his prone body and continued to fire. The scene was gruesome and by the time the robbers fled, both police officers were dead. More than 50 shell casings surrounded their lifeless bodies. A total of $126,500 was stolen.

The largest manhunt in Canadian history ensued. Almost every member of the Montreal Police Department and Quebec Provincial Police was put on the case. In addition, dozens of off-duty constables volunteered to help, while over 40 civil defence workers were recruited to locate the getaway car.

Countless raids were conducted in and around Montreal. Almost all nightclubs, taverns and poolrooms were turned inside out. One unusual development in this search was the co-operation of Montreal's crime bosses. "They are even 'too hot' for us," said one underworld figure to *The Montreal Star.*

On December 19, one day after constables Marineau and Brabant were buried, the first of the three Santa Claus robbery suspects was apprehended. Georges Marcotte was arrested and charged with possessing a revolver and was held at Bordeaux Jail while awaiting trial. Facing the prospect of returning to prison, he attempted to commit suicide but failed. Four days later, police were called to Notre-Dame Hospital when a stroke patient named Jules Reeves was found with $1,297 in cash. Some of the bills matched those stolen. And last but not least, on January 13, 1963, nearly one month after the robbery, Jean-Paul Fournel, the assistant manager of a maternity dress shop, was arrested when the Belgian FN.308 submachine gun used in the crime was found in a garage near his home.

A coroner's inquest was held on January 18, 1963, and Marcotte, Reeves, and Fournel were held criminally responsible for the slayings of the two St-Laurent policemen. At the inquest, Fournel testified that it was Marcotte who had worn the Santa Claus suit, and said that he had later bragged about shooting the policemen. Based on the strength of Fournel's testimony, Marcotte was arraigned on charges of capital murder and sentenced to hang, but Prime Minister Lester B. Pearson later commuted Marcotte's death sentence to life in prison. Marcotte was paroled in 1981 and now lives in Toronto under an assumed name. The building that housed the Canadian Imperial Bank of Commerce branch still stands but is now a flower shop.

**The presence of Prime Minister Trudeau at a parade broke out into a major riot and had Trudeau ducking from a bottle thrown at him. What holiday was being celebrated at the parade?**

➡ **St. Jean Baptiste Day, or the Fête Nationale.** On June 24, 1968, Prime Minister Pierre Trudeau, with a federal election about to take place the following day, chose to attend the annual St. Jean Baptiste Day parade following an invitation by mayor Jean Drapeau.

But the festive occasion would remain anything but festive. Separatist sentiments had been boiling for the past five years and Trudeau's presence at the parade seemed like the perfect opportunity to show their animosity toward him and his federalist policies.

The aftermath of the St. Jean Baptiste Day parade riot was staggering. In addition to 249 arrests and approximately 137 reported injuries, the parade route along Sherbrooke Street was littered with broken glass. In fact, demonstrators had bought bottled soft drinks from concession stands across the street with the sole purpose of using them as missiles. This prompted Montreal Police assistant director Maurice St-Pierre to announce that bottled drinks could no longer be sold along parade routes.

Trudeau was warned against going but chose to ignore his staff's advise. Instead, he spent part of the day making campaign stops across the province, where he was warmly greeted by supporters. At one campaign appearance, he reaffirmed his strong federalist policy regarding Quebec, saying that he was trying "to put Quebec in its place and its place is in Canada and nowhere else". It was comments such as these that enraged separatists.

At 8 p.m., a little over an hour before the start of the parade, trouble started brewing. Over 200 flag-waving, slogan-chanting separatist demonstrators gathered on the corner of Cherrier and Amherst streets. As the number of demonstrators increased, so did the number of Montreal Police Riot Squad personnel called in.

Clashes between police and demonstrators erupted. The demonstrators pelted police with an endless stream of bottles, rocks, and paint-filled containers, and chanted slogans such as "Trudeau to the gallows" and "le Québec aux Québécois" — "Quebec to Quebecers".

Trudeau arrived at 9:30 p.m. and took his seat next to mayor Jean Drapeau and Premier Daniel Johnson. During the course of the parade, Trudeau was met with a series of contrasts. On one float, a group of girls were blowing kisses at him while another shouted "Vive le Québec libre". Trudeau seemed undisturbed by these events. He continued to smile and applaud.

But the disturbances got uglier. The demonstrators managed to halt the parade, threatened to wreck it, overturned three police cars, and set them on fire. When a bottle was tossed into the reviewing stand and smashed harmlessly in the third row of seats, commotion set in and many dignitaries began to flee to safety. Trudeau was urged to leave as well but angrily waved aside the security officers and resumed his seat. Flanked by two security officers, he stayed watching the clashes until the end of the parade at 11 p.m.

Trudeau's symbolic, defiant gesture against the separatists was shown on television news broadcasts across the country, and public opinion was overwhelmingly in Trudeau's favour. A Trudeau associate had this to say about the gesture: "He had done the right thing both in attending and in remaining after trouble started. They said that his view was that he had been invited, accepted the invitation and fulfilled it. Under these circumstances, he felt he had no reason to leave the stand and had an obligation to stay." Trudeau summed it up by saying: "Well, did you expect me to leave?"

And the gesture paid off. The following day, Trudeau won his first federal election with a majority government. However, the 1968 riot put an end to the St. Jean Baptiste Day parade for some time. The parade only resurfaced as part of the Fête Nationale festivities in the 1990s.

**The murder of Hochelaga Bank driver Henri Cleroux on April 1, 1924, led to the hanging of four men, including a popular Montreal police officer. What was the significance of this incident in the annals of Montreal crime?**

➤ **It was the first time that the Montreal underworld came to light with the public.** It all started on the afternoon of April 1, 1924 when an armoured Hochelaga Bank car containing $300,000 in cash was held up by a group of seven armed masked men on the Moreau Street tunnel.

Armed with shotguns, the robbers blasted 12 shots into the car, killing driver Henri Cleroux instantly. A Montreal police constable arrived at the scene immediately, took out Cleroux's gun and fired on the robbers, killing one of them, Harry Stone. Stone's body was found abandoned in a car half an hour after the robbery. Thanks to a list of phone numbers found on him, police arrested Ciro Niero, Joseph Serafini, and his wife Mary at their apartment on Coursol Street. Police arrived to find them counting large piles of money. Another accomplice, Marie Emma Lebeau, was also arrested and charged.

In the days following, the other gang members were also arrested. They were Frank Gambino, Leo Davis, Louis Morel, Mike Valentino, and Tony Frank.

Their trial lasted two days and the jury deliberated for only 11 minutes. All six suspects were found guilty and were sentenced to hang. At 5 a.m. on October 24, 1924, Morel, Gambino, Frank, and Serafini were hung at the Bordeaux Jail. Davis and Valentino had their sentences commuted and were released from Bordeaux in 1939.

An interesting fact in this case was the background of two of the gang members. The first, Louis Morel, who had masterminded the robbery, was a popular Montreal police officer and athlete. But in 1917, Morel was suspended from the police department for his union activities and was dismissed for good when he refused to sever his ties with the policeman's union. He then began drinking and gambling and got involved with the illicit drug trade.

The other, Tony Frank, born Francisco Vincenzia, came to Montreal from Sicily in 1907. He quickly built himself a reputation around Montreal as a "fixer". Always seen at the courthouse dressed in custom-tailored suits, Frank carried large sums of money with him to use as bail for any underworld figures that were arrested.

Frank ran a brothel on Cadieux Street with his second wife and used the money to purchase properties across the city. By the early 1920s, Frank became the undisputed head of the Montreal underworld that, according to author Peter Edwards in his book *Blood Brothers,* "was so powerful that other career criminals paid him a title for the right to commit crimes in his city." It was Frank's wide scope of influence in the Montreal underworld scene that drew Morel and his gang to him to aid them in committing the robbery.

Following the hangings, Supreme Court Justice Louis Coderre completed an investigation of the Montreal Police Department. He discovered that many Montreal policemen were associated with Frank's gang and in fact, were informed in advance of the Moreau Street robbery but did nothing to prevent it.

Although Frank was hung and his gang broken up, organized crime in Montreal continued to flourish.

**The murder of which notorious Montreal underworld gambler in 1946 resulted in a sweeping effort by police to wipe out the city's illegal gambling establishments?**

➥**Harry Davis.** Born in Russia, Davis became a major figure in the Montreal underworld from the 1920s to the 1940s. From his office on Stanley Street in downtown Montreal, he ran a gambling operation worth $200,000 and distributed graft money garnered from the proceeds of his gambling operations to police and city officials.

On an evening in late July of 1946, Davis was approached by Louis Bercowitz, a local mobster wanting to start a gambling establishment of his own. Davis refused his request and soon realized that Bercowitz had not come to request his own business, but to confirm the rumours that Davis had made threats against his life. Davis would not confirm or deny the rumours but did threaten to take care of Bercowitz in the same fashion that he had taken care of Charlie Feigenbaum, a Montreal gangster who had been gunned down in August of 1934 following Feigenbaum's successful efforts to land Davis in jail.

Davis pulled out his revolver and a scuffle between himself and Bercowitz erupted. Bercowitz grabbed the barrel of Davis' gun, drew out his own and fired three shots at Davis who died on the way to the Montreal General Hospital. Shortly after the shooting, Bercowitz surrendered to Montreal Herald columnists Sean Edwin and Al Palmer and gave them a full, detailed confession of the killing, which he claimed was in self-defence. "I am glad I shot him," he boldly declared to the two newspapermen.

The following day, after a 10-minute coroner's inquest, Bercowitz was found criminally responsible for the death of Harry Davis. He was later convicted of manslaughter and sentenced to life in prison.

But the shooting of Harry Davis and the subsequent confession of Louis Bercowitz had further repercussions in the Montreal underworld. On July 29, captain Arthur Tache, head of the Montreal Police Department's Morality Squad, was suspended as a result of charges of irregularities in his

The day after the death of Montreal's underworld gambling boss in July of 1946, an unusual representation of respect occurred at a McGill College Avenue gambling den. While it was doing brisk business, a gunman entered the place and ordered its 50 patrons to clear out, in respect of the fallen Harry Davis. "What's a matter?" said the rather angry gunman. "Don't you think you should show some respect for Harry Davis?" The police later denied any knowledge of the incident.

department. These irregularities included the fact that many of the city's gambling dens got advance notice of upcoming police raids and that many officers were kept in the dark by the police brass about illegal gambling establishments. Tache was replaced by Pacifique Plante, who launched a concentrated effort to wipe out the gambling rackets. This led to the total collapse of the Harry Davis gang and the mass arrest of many of Montreal's leading underworld figures.

However, no matter how sweeping Plante's efforts, gambling establishments in Montreal continued to flourish into the 1950s.

# fROM "CANADA'S FIRST, CANADA'S FINEST" TO THE LAST OF THE TRAMWAYS

## montreal's firsts and lasts

**The headquarters of the Quebec Bank were housed in what Montreal architectural first?**

➡ **The city's first skyscraper.** The eight-storey building at Place d'Armes was Montreal's first true office tower. Construction commenced in 1887 and was completed the following year.

Prior to 1887, no commercial building in the city had risen above five or six storeys due to the lack of elevators (which only appeared in North America in 1850) and the fact that customers were not willing to climb more than six flights of stairs. The construction of the Eiffel Tower in Paris and the Leiter Building in Chicago in the late 1880s proved that tall, sturdy structures could be built with iron and steel. For Montreal's first skyscraper, steel was used for the floors and roof, but the supporting walls (which were 80 to 100 centimetres thick) were made of stone.

This new architectural development sparked major expansion in the Old Montreal historical square known as Place d'Armes. Before 1888, Place d'Armes was not a business centre but was a focal point for public gatherings, parades and processions such as the festivities that commemorated Bishop Ignace Bourget's 50th anniversary as a Roman Catholic clergyman in 1872, and the funeral procession of Sir George-Étienne Cartier, one of the Fathers of Confederation, in 1873. Following the construction of the skyscraper, neighbouring buildings underwent massive renovations and major companies began transferring their head offices to the square, making it the hub of Montreal's business district.

The Quebec Bank skyscraper was originally known as the New York Life Insurance Co. Building and was one of the few buildings in Montreal not constructed with stone from local quarries, but with imported Scottish sandstone, which gave the office tower its distinct red colour. The use of this Scottish sandstone was not the result of a specific demand from the project's architects but was furnished mainly by some enterprising shippers who used the slabs of sandstone as a means of ballast for their empty cargo ships returning to Canada.

Like its architectural counterparts in the United States, Montreal's New York Life Insurance Co. Building had an elevator, a clock tower, and housed a number of professional businesses such as the London and Lancashire Insurance Company, the Quebec Bank, and various legal, engineering, and contractor firms.

Although it now stands much shorter than more modern Montreal skyscrapers such as Place Ville-Marie and the Canadian Imperial Bank of Commerce Building, Montreal's first skyscraper still stands today and houses the Société du Fiducie du Québec, as well as a number of law and architectural firms.

**The murder of Montreal policemen Jules Fortin and Daniel O'Connell in May of 1910, and the subsequent hanging of Timothy Candy, established what Montreal criminal first and last?**

➥**It was the first recorded incident of Montreal policemen killed in the line of duty and, consequently, the last public hanging in Montreal.**

On May 7, 1910, Daniel O'Connell, an off-duty Montreal policeman, was shot in the abdomen when he attempted to intercept a man carrying a bag containing six pairs of rubber boots, and loot valued at $18. Constable Jules Fortin witnessed the event from a streetcar and immediately disembarked to aid the fallen O'Connell. He managed to seize the shooter but could not hold him. He was shot twice and died instantly from a bullet to the temple.

Ironically, the incident occurred only 400 feet from police station #6, where Fortin was posted, on Chaboillez Street between Notre-Dame and St-Jacques. The area was notorious for its frequent street brawls and stabbings and was described as "dank, dismal, dirty and narrow".

O'Connell died later from his wounds. It was the first time that members of the Montreal police force died in the line of duty. Both were unarmed.

Before he died, O'Connell gave his fellow constables a description of the suspect: short, thickset with a heavy grey-brown moustache, sporting a grey shirt, but not wearing a coat or hat. A few days later, a coroner's inquest found Timothy Candy, a 37-year-old ex-sailor and factory worker from Liverpool, England, responsible for the crimes.

Daniel O'Connell was a five-year veteran of the Montreal police force at the time of his murder; he was married and had seven children. Jules Fortin was a newer member of the force, having served only one year. A native of Montmagny, Quebec, Fortin had just returned to work after sustaining an injury while making an arrest, at which time the suspect had slashed his arm with a broken bottle. Fortin was single.

Candy worked as a night watchman at the Ames-Holden Co., where the boots were stolen. He was identified by the owner of a second-hand store to whom Candy had unsuccessfully tried to sell the stolen boots. The store was near the scene of the crime and the owner had witnessed the first shooting. As well, an empty bullet shell that matched the bullet found in Fortin's head was found underneath the desk of a night watchman at the Ames-Holden Co. building. Candy's fate was sealed when bloodstains were found on his vest and shirt. Three days after the crime, on May 10, Candy also broke down and confessed that he had committed the robbery and killed the two constables. He was found guilty of murder and was sentenced to hang.

The execution of Timothy Candy took place in the open courtyard of the Montreal Jail on Delorimier Street on the morning of November 17, 1910. Ever the stoic British military man, Candy was determined to die like a soldier and sailor and showed no fear in the face of death. Pleas were made to spare his life, some ironically coming from Daniel O'Connell's widow who wrote to the Minister of Justice and Governor General Earl Grey for a reprieve, but to no avail.

Candy was hung at 7:57 a.m. and at the jail, a black flag was hoisted up immediately after he was pronounced dead. His last words were "God have mercy on my soul." It was the last time a public hanging took place in Montreal.

**Expo 67 opened with great fanfare and ceremony on April 28, 1967, and hosted the world for six exciting months. Who were the first and last visitors to the Man & His World site?**

→**Al Carter and George Tuttle, respectively.** On April 28, 1967, after five years of diplomacy, negotiations, deadlines, threatened labour disputes, and after the creation of a man-made island from tons of landfill, Expo 67 finally opened its doors to the world.

Along with mayor Jean Drapeau, Quebec Premier Daniel Johnson, Prime Minister Lester B. Pearson, and Governor General Roland Michener, a man named Al Carter, a 45-year-old jazz drummer from Chicago, was at the opening ceremonies at Place des Nations. Carter arrived 24 hours early at the Expo site on Ile Ste. Helene and braved the chilly, windy overnight conditions (along with 25 teenagers) to be the fair's first visitor.

This was not the first time that Carter attempted to be the first visitor at a major event. He had often attempted to reach the turnstile first and had succeeded on many occasions, including the 1962 World's Fair in Seattle.

Carter began working at his task in 1963 by making persistent efforts to contact Expo personnel. He started by writing to mayor Drapeau but never got a reply back. He then contacted other key Expo personnel until he got a letter from admission sales manager Jean-Paul Lussier stating: "If Expo ever issues a certificate for the most persistent and tenacious visitor at the site, the name of Al Carter would be inscribed in gold."

*Items that a visitor to Expo 67 could not be without: a guidebook and a souvenir tray.*

Carter got his wish and, along with being issued Expo passport #00001, received a signed affidavit from assistant area manager Richard Kaufman which said: "This gentleman was waiting at Place d'Accueil this morning at 9:20 for the general public opening. To our knowledge this man is first in line at Expo."

All that persistence was worth the effort and wait for Carter. In a manner befitting of a jazz musician, Carter told *The Gazette:* "I've been at some real swinging fairs before, but this has got to be the best one. I can just feel it, man, it looks great." The success of Expo 67 was immediate. By the end of April, over 1.5 million people had attended.

By the time Expo 67 closed its doors at 2:30 a.m. on opening day, over 335,000 people had visited the site — 200,000 more than anticipated. Crowds were so large that the turnstile computer broke down and the metro line to Ile Ste. Helene had to close briefly, as the system could not handle the large volume of users. The Expo 67 site had 847 buildings, 27 bridges, 30 kilometres of roads and sidewalks, 24,484 parking spaces, and 14,950 trees. Its more than 50 million visitors consumed 5,931,578 hamburgers and 33,500,000 ice cream cones.

Six months later, on October 28, Expo 67 was preparing to close its doors and was eagerly awaiting its 50 millionth visitor. The honour went to Martha Racine, a 39-year-old mother of five from Repentigny, a Montreal suburb, who was paying her 25th visit to Expo. Immediately, Racine and her husband received the red carpet treatment and numerous gifts including a colour television set, a pair of watches, champagne, a commemorative Expo pin set, a book about Expo, a signed commemorative scroll and an all-expense paid two-week trip to Expo 70 in Osaka, Japan.

Expo 67 closed its doors for good at 2 p.m. on October 29, 1967. The final visitor (visitor 50,306,648) was George Tuttle, a 24-year-old philosophy and English student at Sir George Williams University. The excited Calgary native explained his tardiness in getting to Expo 67 by saying: "I got out of bed late."

Unfortunately, Al Carter could not attend the closing ceremonies; he had a gig with his jazz band that night.

**What St-Catherine Street East theatre opened in 1907 as the first venue in Montreal to exclusively show movies?**

→**The Ouimetoscope.** Opened on August 30, 1907, by Leo-Ernest Ouimet, a prominent Montreal film distributor and projectionist, the Grand Ouimetoscope on St-Catherine Street East and Montcalm became the first large-scale theatre in North America built for the sole purpose of showing movies.

Ticket prices at the Ouimetoscope were 10 and 15 cents for matinees, and between 10 and 25 cents for evening screenings. Although there is no record of what moving pictures were shown on that opening day, the theatre featured 12 to 14 movies per day, as well as illustrated songs at every performance — all in English.

Ouimet's project began a year earlier in 1906 when he rented a recital hall called the Salle Poire on the same site to exhibit the moving pictures he was distributing. But when competing movie projectionists began sprouting up in the area and posing a threat, Ouimet decided to buy the Salle Poire, tear it down, and built a larger venue. The Grand Ouimetoscope (or Nationoscope, as it was called in local advertisements) was a much more elaborate theatre with 1,000 seats, a horseshoe-shaped balcony, designed plaster walls, and a seven-piece orchestra, a project which cost a total of $50,000.

From day one, the Grand Ouimetoscope was a success. The day after its opening, *The Gazette* commented that there was a future for this new entertainment medium: "Judging by the attendance at the Nationoscope during the week, moving pictures and illustrated songs are sufficient in themselves to form an entertainment that lasts from two to two and a half hours, and still be interesting enough to induce people to return to the theatre the following week."

Ouimet ran the movie theatre that bore his name until 1915, when he sold it to dedicate more of his efforts to film distribution and production. Fifteen years later, the theatre's name was changed to the Canadien, a name that it kept for 50 years. However, in 1990, its name was changed back to the Ouimetoscope.

The theatre still stands today but according to Dane Lanken in his 1993 book *Montreal Movie Palaces,* the Ouimetoscope building underwent so many transformations "that nothing is recognizable today from the era of Ouimet."

A bronze plaque rests at the site, placed there by the Cinémathèque québécoise in 1966 in recognition of the 60th anniversary of the Ouimetoscope's opening, and to highlight its significance to the history of motion pictures in North America.

## August 29, 1959 was a special day in the history of Montreal's public transit system. Why?

➥ It was the last time that tramways rolled on the streets of Montreal. At 4:12 p.m. on August 29, 1959, the last tramways entered the Mount Royal barns. Consecutively, 175 brand new diesel buses were introduced on eight new and/or extended routes.

The retirement of Montreal's streetcars was the culmination of a $40-million modernization program initiated by the Montreal Transportation Commission (MTC) in 1951. At the time, the city had 937 streetcars and 502 buses, but the tramways (also known as ti-chars by its users) were seen as too slow and inflexible and often clogged motor traffic. Monetarily, they were also too expensive to maintain, costing the MTC over $40 million a year for the upkeep of the tramways and its tracks, as compared to $25,000 a year for the operation and maintenance of a bus. MTC chairman Arthur Duperron, seeing that major cities across North America were scrapping their street railways and inter-urban lines, launched a public transit system modernization program aimed at keeping Montreal's transit system up to date, cost effective, and able to accommodate commuters in rapidly growing suburbs.

 ome of the tramways featured in the parade marking the last day of operations were tramway #2222 (which had been in operation since 1927), tramway #350 (better known as "The Rocket", which in 1892 became Montreal's first electrical streetcar), and trolley bus #3517, built in 1944 and used by the MTC until the final day of operations. The last official passengers to ride Montreal's tramways were Mr. and Mrs. France Maurice, who worked for the MTC for 43 years.

The first step taken was the gradual phasing out of several major downtown tramway routes in 1951. In the summer of 1956, service across the Victoria Bridge was cut and in September of that year, tramways were removed from major west end routes, including the major artery of St-Catherine Street. On August 28, 1959, numerous older streetcars were torched.

*An MTC tramway rolls along McGill Street (circa 1944) 15 years before they were pulled off the streets for good.*

On August 29, thousands of people braved sweltering heat and a thunderstorm to watch the parade marking the last day of operation of the Montreal tramways. The parade was headed by two of the city's trademark observation cars (known for carrying people "ten miles around two mountains") and was ridden by city officials as well as numerous employees and officers dressed in period costume.

The parade contained a convoy of 15 old streetcars and ended with three of the brand new buses being introduced that day. At 4:12 p.m., as the parade ended and the last of the operational streetcars finished their shifts, they were herded into the Mount Royal barns for the last time. The gates were closed by mayor Sarto Fournier and MTC chairman Duperron and "La fin d'une époque. The end of an era" was written in large letters on the gates.

As he closed the gates, mayor Fournier was asked about the prospect that Montreal would get a subway system, seeing as several cities in Germany were experimenting with monorail train systems. Fournier said, rather prophetically: "If they succeed there, I wouldn't be surprised if they are proposed for Montreal." In May of 1962, less than three years after Fournier's statement, construction began on Montreal's subway system, which was completed in October of 1966.

**CFCF Radio became the first commercial radio station in North America when it went to air in 1919. What were the station's original call letters during its early years?**

→**XWA.** The Canadian Marconi Company, which was a division of the Marconi Wireless Telegraph Company, manufactured radios and decided to apply for a broadcasting licence for the sole purpose of selling more Marconi radios and developing a market for them. In 1919, the Federal Department of Naval Services granted the Canadian Marconi Company that licence and established the radio station XWA. Its primitive studios were based in an empty room on the roof of the Marconi plant on William Street in Griffintown, located in the southern part of Montreal.

In the fall of 1919, XWA began transmitting irregular broadcasts to local radio operators. Those first broadcasts were that of announcers doing the "Testing, one, two, three . . ." drill on a regular basis. However, the announcers (plant technicians) often got out of breath from doing these tests repeatedly. Darby Coats, who worked for XWA in its early days, found a solution to this problem. He recommended playing recorded music instead. He borrowed a phonograph and several records from a downtown Montreal music store, and played them in exchange for a promotional announcement. This in turn became the first radio commercial in Canada.

The addition of music to XWA's broadcast schedule proved quite popular. Shortly thereafter, song pluggers and piano companies began supplying free material in exchange for on-the-air publicity. News and weather reports were also added to the broadcasts.

 ome of the programs that aired on CFCF Radio on February 2, 1925, were:

» 12:45 p.m.: Performance by Rex Battle and his Mount Royal Orchestra, live from the Mount Royal Hotel, along with stock reports, weather reports, and time signals.
» 7 p.m.: *Bedtime Stories*.
» 7:30 p.m.: *Dinner Concert* by Joseph C. Smith and his Mount Royal Hotel Dance Orchestra.
» 8 p.m.: Address on physical education by Sidney Chard, physical education director of Montreal's central YMCA.
» 8:30 p.m.: Program of vocal and instrumental music arranged by Edward A. Burrey.
» 10:30 p.m.: Performance by Joseph C. Smith and his Mount Royal Hotel Dance Orchestra.

That same year, the first live talent to appear on XWA was Gus Hill, a popular ballad singer, who performed a repertoire of songs accompanied by legendary Montreal pianist Willie Eckstein.

On November 20, 1920, XWA changed its call letters to CFCF (which stood for Canada's First, Canada's Finest). During its first decade, CFCF was a bilingual radio station and was affiliated with the National Broadcasting Company (NBC). Its French language counterpart, CKAC (founded in 1922) was also bilingual but was affiliated with the Columbia Broadcasting System (CBS). However, because viewers quickly grew tired of the repetition of programming in French and English, CFCF chose to broadcast exclusively in English starting in 1931.

Throughout the 1920s, CFCF's programming would consist mainly of locally produced shows, including big band concerts, dance music, classical music and opera, educational lectures, news, weather, stock market reports, and time signals. In the 1930s, listeners could hear a mix of local and American shows.

There has been a long-standing debate as to whether XWA or KDKA, a Pittsburgh station, presented the first scheduled radio broadcast in North America. "However if a scheduled broadcast is accepted as a starting point, Canada's XWA beat out the American KDKA," wrote Sandy Stewart in his 1985 book *From Coast to Coast.* In May of 1920, XWA relayed a musical program from its studios at the Canada Cement Building to the Château Laurier Hotel in Ottawa for a meeting of the Royal Canadian Society. The program featured a lecture by a McGill University professor, followed by a repertoire of songs by vocalist Dorothy Tulton. It was only in November of that year that KDKA inaugurated its regular schedule of broadcasts when it transmitted the results of the 1920 presidential election between Warren G. Harding and James Cox.

**Before Place des Arts, Her (His) Majesty's Theatre on Guy Street was Montreal's premiere entertainment venue. What was the first show to be presented at Her Majesty's in 1898, and what was its last event in 1963?**

➥ *The Ballet Girl* and a tribute to pianist Willie Eckstein, respectively.

For nearly 65 years, Her (His) Majesty's Theatre was a prominent theatre and concert hall. The 1,800-seat building played host to the best in Broadway, vaudeville, ballet and classical music, and featured such personalities as Lon Chaney, Sarah Bernhardt, the Barrymores, Dave Brubeck, and the famed London-based Gilbert & Sullivan troupe: the D'Oyley Carte Opera Company.

The first stage production at Her Majesty's was a musical entitled *The Ballet Girl*, which opened on November 7, 1898. The attending crowd included prominent Montrealers Sir Hugh Allan, Thomas Roddick, and Montreal mayor Raymond Préfontaine. The proceedings commenced at 8:30 p.m. as mayor Préfontaine addressed the audience, expressing his pride in such a handsome theatre, and explaining how Her Majesty's was proof that Montreal was progressing as a major arts and culture centre. It was followed by a poem recited by a certain Miss May Reynolds who proclaimed:

During its 65 years of existence, Her Majesty's Theatre changed names (from His Majesty's to Her Majesty's, or vice versa) whenever a new monarch was crowned. It became His Majesty's Theatre in 1901, with the death of Queen Victoria and the succession of King Edward VII, and changed back to Her Majesty's Theatre in 1952, with the death of King George VI and the succession of Queen Elizabeth II.

"A few last words, attention! One and all!
And bless the name selected for our hall
It is the noblesse that on Earth is known
It is 'Her Majesty's', we proudly own."

After the orchestra played "God Save the Queen", the production of *The Ballet Girl* began. It received lukewarm reactions. A Montreal Daily Star theatre critic wrote: "A better selection could surely have been made for the opening night . . . Nothing to stamp it as in any way above mediocrity."

By the spring of 1963, Her Majesty's Theatre was showing its age and, with the opening of the 3,000-seat Grande Salle (later Salle Wilfrid-Pelletier) of Place des Arts scheduled for the fall, it was decided that Her Majesty's would close its doors that May.

Some of the last productions shown included the musical *Carnival* (starring American singer/actor Ed Ames), Jean Genest's drama *The Blacks,* and *A Home Is Just for Sleeping,* a satirical revue presented by the Mount Royal Lodge of B'nai Brith Canada in honour of the lodge's 50th anniversary. However, Her Majesty's Theatre brought down the curtain for good with a tribute to Montreal pianist Willie Eckstein.

Known as "the Boy Paderewski", "the World's Greatest Motion Picture Interpreter" and "Mr. Fingers", Eckstein started playing at the age of four and, at the age of 12, turned down a scholarship at the McGill Conservatory of Music to go into vaudeville. From 1912 to 1930, he established his legendary reputation in the Montreal entertainment scene as the resident pianist for the Strand Theatre on St-Catherine Street West and Mansfield.

On May 27, 1963, over 600 people attended the tribute to Eckstein's 70 years in show business at Her Majesty's. The tribute featured stars of stage, television and screen from New York, Chicago and Los Angeles who performed in Eckstein's honour. At midnight, shortly after the show ended, a photographer caught Eckstein walking up the theatre's centre aisle. When he asked Eckstein to look cheerful for a picture, Eckstein told him: "Can't do that. I'm saying goodbye to an old girlfriend."

Thus came to an end Her Majesty's illustrious 65-year history. The following day, *The Montreal Star* wrote: "The lights went out forever last night on the faded curtains and scuffed boards of the old gay lady of Guy Street."

Her Majesty's Theatre was torn down in November of that year. A parking lot now stands in its place.

### On August 11, 1906, Antoine Toutant unwillingly became part of Montreal's automobile history. What happened?

➥**He became Montreal's first auto accident fatality.** At 8:30 p.m., Toutant, a pedestrian, was struck by an oncoming automobile on the corner of St-Catherine and Maisonneuve streets, in the city's east end, with his wife and 14-year-old son watching. He died that same day from a skull fracture.

The car was driven by Herwald Thomas Atkinson, who worked as a chauffeur for the Dominion Park Company (Dominion Park was a popular east end amusement park at the time). At the coroner's inquest held two days later, 15-year-old Alfred St. Charles, who was at the scene and witnessed the accident, described that the car was going at a speed of around 20 to 35 miles per hour, which was "faster than the trotting of a horse". He then saw the car strike Toutant, who hit one of the car's headlights, rolled under the car, and was crushed by one of the wheels.

Atkinson also testified at the inquest and said that he had been driving along the right side of St-Catherine Street when he saw an eastbound streetcar letting off and picking up passengers. He decided to switch to the left side of the road and go around the streetcar. He then told the coroner: "When I got halfway past, the deceased, his wife and another lady, ran across. I swerved to the right to avoid them, blowing my horn at the same time. The deceased and his son stepped out in the way of the auto. The son seemed to hold the father back. As I almost passed through he jumped right in front of the auto, seeming to land on top of the left head lamp."

After Toutant was struck by the car, Atkinson immediately stopped the car and along with Herbert Dalgleish (who was riding with Atkinson), carried the wounded Toutant to a nearby drugstore. They then accompanied him in the ambulance to Notre-Dame Hospital where Toutant was pronounced dead. Atkinson and Dalgliesh were immediately arrested by the police at the hospital. Atkinson was held in jail without bail and was later held criminally responsible for the death of Antoine Toutant. Dalgleish was released before the inquest for lack of evidence.

In the wake of Montreal's first automobile fatality, the Montreal Automobile Club issued a circular, advising its members that horses, not automobiles, were more of a hazard to pedestrians: "An automobile may be stopped within a very few feet, while a horse going at high speed cannot be pulled up in as many yards. Then if a horse gets beyond control through fright or anything of the kind, nothing can stop him, but the automobile depends entirely on the skill and nerve of the driver."

Sadly, the day after Antoine Toutant's tragic death, a second accident involving an automobile and a pedestrian occurred in Montreal. Grace Hill was struck by a car on the corner of St-Catherine and Stanley streets. Although she suffered internal injuries and bruising, her injuries were not fatal.

# the VIEW FROM
# THE MAYOR'S CHAIR

## the colourful characters who held
## the title of mayor of montreal

**Jacques Viger, Montreal's first mayor, was responsible for the design of the city's coat of arms in 1833. What Latin motto is found on the coat of arms, and what does it stand for in English?**

➥ **"Concordia Salus", which means "salvation through harmony."** Adopted by Viger, Montreal's coat of arms was passed by city council on July 18, 1833. In addition to the motto, the seal shows the symbols of the four groups who helped settle and develop Montreal: the rose (English), thistle (Scottish), shamrock (Irish), and fleur-de-lys (French).

Besides being the city's first mayor and being responsible for its coat of arms, Viger contributed significantly to the growth of Montreal as a city. A journalist by trade, Viger fought with de Salaberry's Voltigeurs during the War of 1812 and, in 1813, was named Montreal's roads and bridges inspector. In 1825, Viger introduced Montreal's first census.

ontreal's first city council members were: Jacques Viger, John Donegani, William Forbes, Joseph Gauvin, Alexander Lusignan, John McDonnell, Robert Nelson, Charles-Séraphin Rodier, Joseph Roy, John Torrance, Augustin Tullock, John Turney, Guillaume J. Vallée, François Derome, Mahum Hall, Julius Perrault, and Turton Penn. Total annual mayoral wages in 1833: $400.

The City of Montreal was officially incorporated by the royal assent of King William IV of England on April 12, 1832. In May of 1833, a group of justices of the peace announced that June 5 would be an election day where Montreal would elect its first city council and mayor. A special committee of 1,300 men, primarily property owners, conducted the election. By hand votes, these 1,300 men elected 16 councillors to represent eight electoral districts.

The next task was to elect the city's first mayor. Viger, who at the time was committee secretary, was chosen by 13 of the 16 councillors.

Viger's administration, besides adopting the city seal, also improved the city's street lighting, adopted preventive measures against cholera, and introduced a drainage system for the city's suburb-like districts (known as "faubourgs").

However, his administration was also tainted with controversy. Viger, a cousin of Louis-Joseph Papineau, leader of the Patriotes, was a sympathizer of his cause. In 1834, he presided over the very first St. Jean Baptiste Day celebrations held to protest British tyranny in Lower Canada and to support Papineau's 92 Resolutions. By 1836, Montreal was seething in dissatisfaction and turbulence, which later erupted in the Rebellion of Lower Canada.

Due to the explosive political climate in the city, the Governor General decided to dissolve city council and not renew the city's charter, and Viger lost his post as mayor. The next mayor to be elected was Peter McGill in 1840.

## Who was the first mayor to be elected by popular vote?

➥ **Charles Wilson.** In 1851, Montreal's city council passed a statute that allowed the office of mayor of Montreal to be elected by the public at large. Nineteen years earlier, when the city was incorporated, the mayor was voted by the 16 city councillors, who in turn were elected by male citizens meeting the following qualifications: were over the age of 21, possessed real estate in the city, and had been living on this real estate for the past 12 months.

Wilson, who was born in Scotland, ran a successful hardware business and served as director of the Scottish Provincial Assurance Company. During his two-year term as mayor, Wilson advocated that the rich pay back taxes, raised enough revenue to help build Montreal's first City Hall (which later became Bonsecours Market), and launched the first transatlantic steamer service.

Perhaps the sole incident that forever marked Wilson's administration was the Gavazzi Riot. Alessandro Gavazzi, an ex-Roman Catholic monk from Italy, toured the United States and Britain delivering a series of anti-papal lectures that were met with a great degree of success. However, the predominantly Roman Catholic Quebec society was not ready to receive Gavazzi and his lectures. A riot broke out when he lectured in Quebec City on June 6, 1853. His stop in Montreal produced similar effects.

The lecture took place at the Zion Church at Haymarket (Victoria) Square. Policemen were stationed outside the church and successfully prevented an angry group of Catholic Irishmen from storming the church. However, shots were fired, which led to confusion and a hasty conclusion to Gavazzi's lecture. A small military detachment called the Cameronians (the Cameron Highlanders) were outside the church and also fired shots after mayor Wilson unsuccessfully read the Riot Act. By the time it was over, 40 people were killed or wounded and two women were almost trampled to death. Gavazzi escaped from the incident unharmed.

The Riot Act is read if a high-ranking public official (such as a mayor, judge or sheriff) assesses, at a site in question, that a riot will erupt. He demands silence and reads aloud this passage before handing over control of the city to its police force for 24 hours: "Her Majesty the Queen charges and commands all persons being assembled immediately to dispense and peaceably to depart to their habitations or to their lawful business upon the pain of being guilty of an offence for which, upon conviction, they may be sentenced to imprisonment for life. God save the Queen."

Although it was never known who gave the order to fire upon the attendees, mayor Wilson was the one accused. He quickly denied it. On June 26, 1853, an investigation was conducted. It ended inconclusively and no arrests were made, although many people thought that the affair was hushed up by Wilson as a political move.

## Who was the only Montreal mayor to serve as Prime Minister of Canada?

➥Sir John Abbott. He was chosen to be Prime Minister after Sir John A. Macdonald's death on June 6, 1891, just a few months after Macdonald won a sixth mandate as prime minister in the federal election earlier that year.

Born in the town of St-André-Est in Lower Canada on March 12, 1821, John Joseph Caldwell Abbott has the distinction of being the first Canadian-born prime minister. His career began in Montreal, where he was a distinguished lawyer and politician. He served as dean of McGill University's Faculty of Law and was a federal Member of Parliament for the riding of Argenteuil from 1859 to 1867.

The Pacific Scandal in a nutshell: In 1873, Abbott was serving as lawyer for Montreal millionaire/businessman Sir Hugh Allan. In February of that year, while Abbott was away in England, a confidential clerk rifled through his papers and found some vital and damaging documents, which he sold to the opposing Liberal Party. One of these documents included a telegram sent by Sir John A. Macdonald and Sir George-Étienne Cartier to Abbott, which demanded $10,000 from Allan to help finance the building of the Canadian Pacific Railway (CPR). In return for the money, Allan was awarded the lucrative contract to build the CPR. The Liberals revealed the scandal to the public in April of 1873 and Macdonald stepped down as prime minister six months later.

Abbott was a strong supporter of the federal Conservative Party. However, his political career came to a standstill in the 1870s when he became involved in the Pacific Scandal, which led to Macdonald's resignation from office in 1873.

He returned to politics in 1880 when he was re-elected to the House of Commons. Seven years later, he was also elected mayor of Montreal by a 2,000 vote margin, and was acclaimed the following year for another term.

His contributions while in office were significant. Primarily, Abbott convinced the city to donate a suitable piece of land on the slopes of Mount Royal to build a hospital that would welcome Montreal's sick, regardless of race and creed. In support, prominent Montreal businessmen Lord Strathcona and George Stephen donated $1 million to build this hospital, which became the Royal Victoria Hospital, named in honour of Queen Victoria's golden jubilee. Built on 18 acres and based on a Scottish baronial castle, the Royal Victoria Hospital also became a medical research centre and training ground for nurses and McGill medical students.

Mayor Abbott also introduced the practice of voting by secret ballot during civic elections, which was used for the first time in the 1889 municipal elections. During his two terms as mayor, Abbott also held the positions of senator, government leader in the Senate, and minister without portfolio in the Macdonald government.

Abbott finished his term as mayor in 1889, when he followed City Hall's tradition of stepping down after serving two years in the mayor's chair (he was succeeded by Jacques Grenier). In June of 1891, the 70-year-old Abbott was in ill health but enjoying life in his mansion on Sherbrooke and Stanley streets. As one of Montreal's most prominent

*An early portrait of Sir John Abbott, Mayor of Montreal from 1887 to 1889 and Prime Minister of Canada from 1891 to 1892.*

lawyers, the last thing Abbott wanted was to be Prime Minister of Canada. However, as Sir John A. Macdonald lay dying, he became the Conservative Party's choice to take office while anointed successor Sir John Thompson had a chance to prove himself in the House of Commons. According to the late Montreal historian Edgar Andrew Collard, Abbott was "someone without any personal ambitions that might incline him to hold on . . . a man of broad experience and high abilities, fit to be a Prime Minister, but willing to be only a temporary figure on the scene."

Abbott fit the bill. Shortly after Macdonald's death, he was named Canada's third prime minister. Abbott administered from his seat in the Senate, which allowed Thompson to distinguish himself in the Commons and set himself up as his successor. Abbott ran government with skill and firm resolution and passed a number of astute policies, yet never delivered a speech in public. In short, the Abbott government was a success. But Abbott's frail health forced him to step down as prime minister on December 2, 1892, after serving only 18 months. He died in October of 1893 and is buried in Montreal's Mount Royal Cemetery.

## Who served the shortest term (four months) as mayor of Montreal?

→**Francis Cassidy.** Born in 1827 in the village of Saint-Jacques de l'Achigan, Cassidy studied law at Assomption College and was admitted to the bar in 1848. He became a lawyer for the Crown in 1863 and later opened his own law firm in Montreal County.

Cassidy was known as one of the most brilliant civil lawyers in Montreal and handled a number of celebrated cases. One of his most notorious was the Guibord Affair in 1869, in which the Roman Catholic Church and Montreal Archdiocese Bishop Ignace Bourget forbade the burial at the Catholic Cote des Neiges Cemetery of Joseph Guibord, a printer who angered the church by refusing to give up his membership at the Institut Canadien, an organization that promoted liberal thought and ideology. The legal battles lasted until 1875 at which point the London Supreme Court ruled against the church and allowed the proper Catholic burial of Guibord's body. Cassidy, himself a member of the Institut from 1858 to 1867, defended Guibord's widow to ensure that her late husband had a proper Catholic burial.

Cassidy also served as president of the St. Patrick's Society, a benevolent society founded in 1834 that aided Montreal's growing Irish community (and that also organized the annual St. Patrick's Day Parade).

*Prominent Montreal lawyer Francis Cassidy, who served the shortest term as Montreal mayor, from March to June of 1873.*

He began his career in politics in 1871 when he was elected by acclamation to the Quebec legislative assembly as the representative for the Montreal-Ouest riding. Sir John A. Macdonald later offered him the post of federal solicitor general, which he turned down.

Cassidy also had some brief experience in municipal affairs. He was elected to Montreal's city council in 1865 and served one term as councillor. On March 10, 1873, Francis Cassidy was elected the 14th mayor of Montreal by acclamation. Ill health did not allow Cassidy the opportunity to fully perform his mayoral duties as he was too ill to deliver his inaugural address after his election. He worked at City Hall only two or three times per week and only presided over two council meetings. His career as mayor was cut short when he died from a heart ailment on June 14, 1873, only four months after taking office. He was succeeded by Aldis Bernard.

Francis Cassidy's last words, according to *The Montreal Star,* were to a fellow lawyer just a few days before his death. "Well — I am going where there will be no pleas or motions, only judgements."

**During the night of March 3, 1922, mayor Mederic Martin was awakened with news that would send him rushing to City Hall. What was this announcement?**

➡**That City Hall was engulfed in flames that would most likely destroy the entire building and its contents.**

It was shortly after midnight when a fire broke out in the basement of City Hall, near the furnace room located directly under the central core of the building. In less than 24 minutes, the flames had spread upward through the main section of the building and were coming through the roof, creating a pillar of flames and smoke that went as high as 60 feet above the tallest tower of the building.

A general alarm was called and almost every Montreal Fire Department fire engine company was pressed into service. But there was little they could do. The flames were ferocious and were spreading quickly. By 2:10 a.m., all the towers had collapsed and the only thing left for firemen to do was to try and contain the blaze and protect adjacent buildings.

Numerous passersby watched the spectacle in amazement. *The Montreal Daily Star* reported: "The fire produced a beautiful spectacle the

*Montreal City Hall the morning after it was totally destroyed by a fire on March 3, 1922. It took nearly four years to rebuild it.*

sight of which was not given to near-by residents alone but to all within a radius of many city districts. The glare of the flames made an enormous reflection in the sky which, owing to the fact that it occurred at night and in a particularly dark corner of the downtown district, lighted up the entire neighborhood."

Although several firemen suffered minor injuries (one was seriously injured by a piece of falling glass), the main concern was for City Hall's enormous collection of historical documents, art treasures, and civic documentation records. Mayor Martin, who had just returned from Quebec City, was about to go to bed that night when he received news of the fire. He rushed to City Hall and instructed Montreal Fire Chief Chevalier to do whatever he could to save the section of the building that housed the vaults containing the city's records. Martin then turned his attention to his personal papers and dashed into the burning building to his second-floor office to try and retrieve them. Drenched by the water from the fire hoses and stifled by the smoke, he had to turn back. He attempted a second time by placing a ladder at his office window but only made it halfway up when firemen warned him of the impending danger of the tower collapsing. Martin climbed down, took refuge in the pilot's seat of a fire truck located on Notre-Dame Street, and watched as his chambers and the rest of City Hall went up in flames.

However, police sergeant Ferdinand Lafleur, one of mayor Martin's personal attendants, braved the fire and smoke and, crawling on his hands and knees, managed to get into the mayor's office, located his papers and brought them out intact, along with the mayor's gold chain of office.

At 8:53 a.m., nearly nine hours after the blaze started, the fire engine bells rang the "all out" signal. Montreal City Hall, built in 1878 and modelled after Paris' City Hall, was totally destroyed. Martin estimated the damage to the building and its valuable collection of documents and art to between $500,000 and $10 million.

Martin asserted that the city's business would continue nonetheless. Some papers located in the underground vaults were saved. When asked by *The Montreal Daily Star* about the prospect that some of

The newly built Montreal City Hall was officially opened on February 15, 1926. However, Martin was not present for the dedication. He was defeated by Charles Duquette in the 1924 municipal election. Martin would be re-elected mayor in the 1926 election, and only then would he have the opportunity to preside in the mayor's chair of the new City Hall that he helped rebuild.

Montreal's single men would try to dodge payment of the city's bachelor tax because the documentation might have been destroyed in the fire, he replied: "Nothing doing. The records of taxation are all kept in the vaults which are fireproof, and you may count on it they are safe".

## Who was the only Montreal mayor to be arrested while in office?

➡**Camillien Houde.** On August 2, 1940, Houde informally told a group of reporters that he would refuse to obey the law that required Canadians over the age of 16 to register for possible war service. Believing that it would lead to conscription, Houde also recommended that the good citizens of Montreal follow his example and refuse to register.

Campbell Carroll, a City Hall reporter for *The Gazette,* typed up the statement and, on the orders of city editor Tracey Luddington, brought it to Houde who cheerfully signed it. It was published the next day. When federal government censor Eddie McMahon got wind of the story, he forbade *The Gazette* to publish the story again, stating the wartime censorship measure. To get around this censorship measure, Gazette president John Bassett called federal Conservative Party leader Richard Bedford Bennett and dictated the story to him over the phone. Bennett then read it aloud in the House of Commons the following day. The statement was duly entered into the parliamentary records and, as a result, the story could no longer be censored.

Houde's refusal to register sent shock waves across the country. On August 5, 1940, he was arrested by Royal Canadian Mounted Police officers for breaching the Defence of Canada Regulations. Houde was

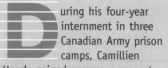

**D**uring his four-year internment in three Canadian Army prison camps, Camillien Houde gained enormous respect from his fellow internees. Despite performing basic, menial tasks at the camps, Houde excelled at wood chopping, Chinese checkers, and long-distance skating. According to Houde, who put in long hours at City Hall when he was mayor, "it was the only holiday I ever had".

stripped of his title of mayor and was replaced by Adhemar Raynault. He spent the next four years in internment camps on Ile Ste. Helene in Montreal, Petawawa, Ontario, and in Fredericton, New Brunswick.

He was released on August 16, 1944, and was given a hero's welcome by over 10,000 people at Central Station upon his return to Montreal the following day. Houde never apologized for his anti-conscription statement, feeling, according to author William Weintraub in his book *City Unique,* that it would "destroy his credibility among all those voters who adored his impudence." On the other hand, he also never held a grudge against *The Gazette,* whose publication of the story led to his arrest.

Houde ran again for the position of mayor in November of 1944 and won, defeating the incumbent Raynault. He remained mayor of Montreal until 1954 and never registered for conscription.

**Which two candidates were at the heart of Montreal's dirtiest and most bitterly fought mayoral election in 1957, which involved ballot box stuffing, intimidation, vandalism, and telegraphing, a method in which an individual appeared at a polling station using another voter's name?**

↪ **Jean Drapeau and senator Sarto Fournier.**

Since winning the mayoralty three years prior in 1954, Jean Drapeau had made many enemies. During his first three years in office, from 1954 to 1957, Drapeau decided to conduct what he called a "public morality clean-up". This involved trying to clean up the city and City Hall from rampant corruption and tolerance of vice, such as gambling and prostitution.

His main enemy was Quebec Premier Maurice Duplessis. The major sticking point between the two was the Dozois Plan, which proposed the clearing of 10 blocks of the city's worst slums in central Montreal and the replacement of these slums with low-cost housing units. Drapeau was

I SHALL NOT SERVE

This is an all-important message to the people of Montreal on the eve of the civic elections.

It is a message which no Montreal elector can afford to neglect.

At the very opening of his campaign, and on several occasions since, Jean Drapeau has made it clear that he will not serve a second term as mayor, even if he is elected, unless he seizes control of city council and the executive committee.

There are two obvious fallacies in this statement. The first is that no one, not even Jean Drapeau, can dictate how the people must vote. Such orders may have their place in Soviet Russia, but not in a democracy.

The second fallacy is that there is no possibility that Jean Drapeau's clique will win a majority in council. The people of Montreal want a new deal in municipal affairs — an administration of justice instead of vindictiveness. The Civic Action League, as a voice in city government, is through.

The fact that emerges from Jean Drapeau's assertion, therefore, is that if he himself is re-elected — and that is most doubtful — he will leave the city without a mayor.

Montreal has had enough crises in the administration of its affairs in the past three years. It cannot risk the possibility of further difficulties in the coming three years.

**A VOTE FOR JEAN DRAPEAU IS A WASTED VOTE**

Montreal can get the administration it deserves only by voting for Senator Sarto Fournier for the mayoralty, and for all the candidates of the Greater Montreal Rally.

These standard-bearers of the GMR will administer Montreal as it should be administered.

*They will administer. They will not crush.*

**GREATER MONTREAL RALLY**

Headquarters: AVenue 8-6335    Central Committee: 4177 St. Denis — PLateau 9064*

*A vicious anti-Drapeau newspaper advertisement placed by Sarto Fournier's Greater Montreal Rally party (October 1957).*

vehemently opposed to the plan while Duplessis supported it. Duplessis won.

The situation did not improve for Drapeau. The Montreal underworld was unhappy with his crackdown on their narcotics and gun-running operations. Many people involved in these illicit operations were angry that they were losing money rapidly. Drapeau also made many enemies when he dismissed 200 city garbagemen before Christmas of 1956 and tried to also dismiss the Montreal police chief, whom he proved was corrupt. This last decision was overturned by the Quebec Superior Court.

With Duplessis' quiet support, a new political party was created to face off against Drapeau in the 1957 municipal election, a party called the Greater Montreal Rally (GMR). Its leader was senator Sarto Fournier.

From the start, the 1957 election campaign was a bitter, violent campaign. Constant stories of violence, vandalism, intimidation, negative campaign literature and strangers appearing at polling stations on behalf of legitimately registered voters, a practice known as telegraphing, were reported.

And as the campaign progressed into the final weeks, things got even uglier. When Drapeau stated that he would not accept another mandate as mayor unless he had total control of both the council and the executive committee, the GMR placed advertisements in Montreal newspapers with the headline "I shall not serve" showing Drapeau giving a Nazi salute.

On October 26, individuals entered the office of GMR candidate Harvey Goldman on Van Horne Avenue and tore up tabulation sheets, scattered papers, stole 35,000 voter cards, and turned over several tables and typewriters. Numerous ballot boxes and voters' lists were also stolen throughout the course of the elections.

Things did not improve come October 28, election day. Although things started rather quietly when the polls opened at 8 a.m., trouble began brewing as the day progressed. The Montreal Police Department assigned 566 special constables to help maintain order.

A total of 30 people were arrested for telegraphing, of which 19 were detained for carrying false identification cards (which were held until the polls closed). A ballot box was stolen from a polling station on Lajeunesse Street, one deputy returning officer was short 58 ballot slips at his poll, and a police car stopped a vehicle containing four suspected strong-arm men. Eight more suspicious cars were identified.

Polls closed at 7 p.m. and Duplessis' candidate Sarto Fournier prevailed. However, Drapeau's Civic Action League (CAL) held the balance of power at City Hall, with 33 councillors elected compared to 21 for the GMR.

Drapeau spent his three years out of office organizing his comeback. Starting in 1958, he made several public speaking appearances at $1 per person (in both French and English) in which he stated that the mayoralty was taken away from him, and criticizing Fournier and his policies. As well, he severed his ties to the CAL and created a new party, the Civic Party of Montreal. It all paid off in 1960 when he was re-elected. He served until his retirement in 1986.

**In 1968, mayor Drapeau introduced a lottery that would help pay the debt accumulated for Expo 67. What was this lottery better known as?**

→ **The Voluntary Tax.**

In April of 1968, as a result of building the metro and hosting Expo 67, the City of Montreal was faced with a huge cost of living bill, which exceeded $285 million, and a deficit of nearly $40 million for the 1968–1969 fiscal year.

To alleviate this deficit and help balance the upcoming municipal budget, mayor Drapeau announced a new scheme to city council that he called the Voluntary Tax Assessment. The plan was simple. People would voluntarily donate $2 per person, an amount that would lead to a major cash payoff if they correctly answered a skill-testing question once their ticket number was drawn. Over $150,000 in cash prizes would be awarded each month, including a grand prize of $100,000. Drapeau expected the Voluntary Tax to bring in revenues of $32 million per year, which would help to ease the city's deficit. Without it, the city would have to impose a 20 percent tax hike. Montreal's city council passed this recommendation unanimously and the first draw was scheduled for May 20, 1968.

Montreal became the first community in Canada to have a $2 voluntary tax system. Montrealers responded positively to the tax and, within days of its announcement, the mayor received over 700 letters containing $2 bills.

Perhaps the most vocal opponent to the Voluntary Tax was veteran city councillor Frank Hanley, who had argued in favour of a legalized lottery in Montreal to benefit the poor as early as 1948, and who called Drapeau's scheme "a disgusting about-face".

Hanley angrily told *The Montreal Star* that "now the moralist, the man who with [former Montreal Police Vice Squad head] Pax Plante closed down gambling in every form, including church bingoes . . . Now this scourge of gambling calls on Montrealers and the world at large to support a lottery."

Drapeau adamantly told his critics that his Voluntary Tax was not a lottery, arguing that there was nothing illegal about it because successful candidates would get their cash prizes solely on the basis of correctly answering the skill-testing question.

In addition, Montreal's Voluntary Tax program was put together without Premier Daniel Johnson's knowledge, and the provincial government predicted that it would not work. According to a government spokesman, the lottery would be a "trick that will fall through".

Although it did not help substantially with the reduction of the city's debt, the Voluntary Tax became an immediate hit with the public. The Quebec government, who thought it would not last and later challenged Drapeau's plan in court and lost, later adopted the Voluntary Tax to establish Loto Quebec, the province's first lottery, in 1970.

During his 18 years as mayor of Montreal, Camillien Houde developed a legendary reputation for his quick wit, sense of humour and colourful remarks. When King George VI and Queen Mary were at City Hall during their historical visit in May of 1939, what did Houde tell the Queen when the Royals acknowledged the cheering crowds from a balcony?

➡ He said "You know, Your Majesty, some of those cheers are for you also."

In a political career that lasted almost 30 years on all three levels of government, Houde became known for the flamboyant, jovial manner he carried out his duties, whether as leader of the Quebec Conservative Party, as a provincial MNA, a federal Member of Parliament, or especially, as mayor of Montreal. His boisterous laughter and glib sense of humour generated a whole collection of remarks that made him a favourite of the press and a much sought-after guest speaker. A few examples of the Houde sense of humour include:

» Twelve years after the royal visit, Houde played host to two other members of the British royal family, Princess Elizabeth and Prince Phillip. At a gala dinner in the princess' honour, Houde said to her: "I am very pleased, Your Royal Highness, to be your host at dinner this evening. As you may have heard, I was the guest of your father for four years until recently" (referring to the four-year period from 1940 to 1944 when he was arrested and interred for his outright public refusal to support the federal government's program of conscription into the armed forces).

*Mayor Camillien Houde (right) being the perfect host to Princess Elizabeth and Prince Phillip (1951).*

» According to one well-circulated urban legend about the mayor, Houde committed an unintentional linguistic gaffe during the 1949 Grey Cup game in Toronto between the Montreal Alouettes and the Calgary Stampeders. Given the honours of performing the ceremonial opening kickoff, Houde addressed the crowd at Varsity Stadium and said, in his unique command of the English language, that he had the honour to "kick your balls".

» During a question and answer period following a speech that he gave in Ottawa in December of 1953, Houde was asked what made Montreal such an attractive city. He replied: "We keep a nice balance between the praying and the sinning."

» At a speech a year earlier, Houde read off a list of all the ethnic communities that made up the population of Montreal. When he finished, he added: "I hope I haven't left any out. There is an election coming."

» In February of 1954, as Houde's political career was coming to an end, Premier Maurice Duplessis, with the unanimous consent of the entire Quebec National Assembly, proposed an annual pension for Houde, which would equal approximately two-thirds of his annual salary as mayor (which was $18,000 at the time). Houde, who was present in the assembly chamber during the discussion, left before the vote took place. When he returned following the vote, Duplessis told him that the assembly had voted against Houde's pension. "I am surprised to hear that," expressed Houde. "There are so many around who would like to get rid of me."

With such a quick wit, it is not surprising that Houde was a member of an entertainer's union!

## What was significant about Montreal brewer Henry Archer Ekers, who served as mayor from 1906 to 1908?

→**He was the last anglophone Montreal mayor.** A brewer by trade, Ekers was born in Montreal on September 8, 1855. His father, Thomas Ekers, founded the Ekers Brewery in which Henry started working at the age of 14. Known for his natural aptitude for business, for his energy and foresight, young Henry was quickly appointed the brewery's manager.

Besides running a successful brewery, Ekers also had a nose for politics, especially civic politics, and worked hard for the cause of education in the city. Municipal politics seemed to run in the family; his grand uncle Thomas Phillips was one of the first Montreal aldermen and served in the administration of Peter McGill (who was the city's first anglophone mayor).

ike brewer Henry Ekers, the 40 men elected as mayor of Montreal came from various backgrounds. Here are a few of their pre-mayoral occupations:

» Édouard-Raymond Fabre (1849–1851): bookseller
» William Hales Hingston (1875–1877): doctor
» Raymond Préfontaine (1898–1902): lawyer
» Louis Payette (1908–1910): construction developer
» Fernand Rinfret (1932–1934): journalist
» Pierre Bourque (1994–2002): horticultural engineer

Ekers followed in his uncle's footsteps in 1898, when he was first elected as an alderman for the St. Lawrence Ward. He was then appointed to the Civic Finance Committee and was dedicated to having the city's business run like a business, as well as wanting to straighten out the city's finances, which were in a poor state. At the time, the city was $1 million in debt due to outstanding payments owed to the city by several large firms. Ekers forced those firms in question to pay up, which they did.

As an alderman, Ekers despised municipal schemes that shamefully wasted taxpayers' money. As well, he fought against mishandled city projects, especially when they cost the city a great deal of money.

Establishing a reputation as a reformer at City Hall who cleaned up municipal politics, Ekers ran for mayor in 1906, during which time he waged a hard-fought campaign against W.E. Doran, who unsuccessfully ran for the mayoralty in 1904. Doran believed that it was time for an Irish-born mayor, advocated early closings of saloons, the strict enforcement of licences and other laws, as well as cheap water and electricity rates. Ekers campaigned on the principles of Canadianism and used his impressive record as an alderman and reformer. The campaign even had its moments of dirty tricks, when women and children were pressed into service to go around the city and spread rumours that would malign Ekers' character.

With the endorsement of his departing fellow aldermen (as well as several of Montreal's protective and benevolent societies), Ekers defeated Doran by a margin of 3,443 votes. The local press enthusiastically welcomed the brewer's election to the mayor's chair. "It was pretty conclusively shown by the electorate that when an alderman serves the city honestly for many years, it is remembered, and that in due course a reward for the same will be given," said *The Montreal Daily Star* the day after the February 1, 1906 municipal election.

During his administration, Ekers faced several important issues such as the annexation of municipalities, improving city streets, burying overhead wires, reducing water rates and increasing real estate taxes to counter a $28 million city debt. However, he ran City Hall with the same business ability, dignity and tact that he employed as a brewer and alderman.

When Ekers left office in 1908, the unwritten civic tradition of alternating between English and French-speaking mayors ended. No anglophone has served as Montreal's mayor since.

Ekers returned to the family brewery business and became Director of National Breweries. He retired in 1921 and died on February 1, 1927, at the age of 71. The Ekers Brewery building, located on St. Lawrence Boulevard, now serves as the headquarters for the Just for Laughs comedy festival.

# CITY OF
## CHAMPIONS

## montreal's proud sports traditions recalled

The 1919 Stanley Cup final between the Montreal Canadiens and the Seattle Metropolitans was the only final series to end undecided at two games apiece. What tragic circumstances caused this deadlock, leaving neither team to be declared winners of the Stanley Cup?

→**The Spanish Influenza,** which led to the death of one of the members of the Canadiens.

It all began well. In Seattle, the Canadiens and Metropolitans played four exciting games. Newsy Lalonde scored all four Habs' goals in Game 2, and Game 4 ended in a scoreless tie after one hour and 40 minutes of overtime play. However, things seemed to change in Game 5 when many of the players appeared fatigued and drained. Joe Hall, the Habs' right defenceman, left the game early. The game was completed but five other Habs members (Odie Cleghorn, Newsy Lalonde, Louis Berlinguette, Jack McDonald and manager George Kennedy) caught the flu and were sent to bed. By April 6, all were gradually recovering from their illness, all except for Hall, whose condition turned for the worse. While in critical condition at a Seattle hospital, he contracted pneumonia. He died that day at 3 p.m.

Born in England, (Mean) Joe Hall was known as the Bad Man of Hockey and was a drawing card for the Canadiens. However, his nickname was misleading because, off the ice, he had a warm and sunny disposition and ran his own cigar business during off-season.

"He never spared himself, and though he was rough at times, this was usually in retaliation for offences his opponents had committed," said

*The Montreal Daily Star* the day after his death. Frank Patrick, president and coach of the Pacific Coast Hockey Association's Vancouver Millionaires at the time, remembered Hall as "one of the real veterans of hockey . . . off the ice he was one of the jokiest, best-hearted, most popular men who ever played."

A 15-year professional hockey veteran, Hall led the Quebec Bulldogs to Stanley Cup championships in 1912 and 1913, and joined the Canadiens in 1917 when the Bulldogs' franchise folded. He lived in Brandon, Manitoba, and left behind a wife and three children.

As a result of the influenza epidemic that infected several of the Habs and led Joe Hall to his death, the 1919 Stanley Cup final was cancelled in a 2–2 deadlock. To this day, no winner has been declared.

**The 1931 Grey Cup game between the Montreal AAA Winged Wheelers and the Regina Rough Riders was not only the first Grey Cup championship to be won by a Montreal-based team but also introduced a frequently used football technique. Which technique was this?**

➡**The forward pass.** It was introduced by the Winged Wheelers' quarterback Warren Stevens, who successfully threw 3 out of 11 forward passes in a lopsided 22–0 victory over the Regina Rough Riders at the 1931 Grey Cup game (or, as it was called at the time, the Dominion Championship Final) at McGill Stadium.

The Canadian Rugby Union convened several Canadian football leagues for a meeting on February 2, 1931. Here, the forward pass was officially adopted. But its adoption was not a quick one. Although each football league was in favour of it, each league had a different view and interpretation of what defined the forward pass, and each wanted to word the rule differently. The Western League wanted all offensive players to receive the pass; the Ontario Rugby Football Union (ORFU) wanted to duplicate the American rules (in which the ball was thrown forward in the direction of the opponent's goal line), while the intercollegiate and interprofessional unions favoured the western-style rules (where the ball could be thrown forward toward the opponent's dead line, which was 25 yards behind and parallel to the goal line).

Football teams across the country readily accepted this new innovation in the game. The Montreal AAA Winged Wheelers were the first eastern team to score a touchdown using the forward pass on October 10, 1931, in a 32–6 victory over the Ottawa Roughriders. And when Montreal and Regina faced each other for the 1931

If you think spending hundreds of dollars for a Grey Cup ticket is steep today, consider these ticket prices for the 1931 game, which was played during the height of the Great Depression: $1.50 and $2 for reserved seats, $1 for general admission, and 25 cents for children under the age of 18.

Grey Cup on the frozen solid gridiron of McGill Stadium, both teams used the forward pass as a major part of their respective game plans. But it wasn't until the third quarter of the game, when Warren Stevens threw a 40-yard pass to Kennie Grant, that the first forward pass touchdown in Grey Cup history was recorded. It was the Winged Wheelers' 14th straight victory and the first Grey Cup championship ever won by a Montreal based team. For the Rough Riders, it was their third Grey Cup loss in four years (losing in 1928 and 1930 as well).

**Pennant fever swept Montreal in the fall of 1981 as the Montreal Expos faced the Los Angeles Dodgers in the National League Championship Series. However, the Expos' dream of making their first World Series appearance was dashed by a home run from Dodger Rick Monday in Game 5. Who delivered that fateful pitch and what colourful nickname is this game now remembered as?**

➥**Steve Rogers and Blue Monday, respectively.** Rogers, who was the ace of the Expos' starting pitcher rotation, had an incredible October during the strike-divided 1981 season. Since the end of the player's strike that August, his win-loss record was 7–4, he had a 1.63 ERA, and allowed only one run in 26 and two-thirds innings.

On October 2, Rogers pitched a two-hit shutout against the New York Mets to win the National League East Division title for the second half of the season. Nine days later, Rogers' prowess on the mound continued, as his six-hit, 3–0 shutout against the Philadelphia Phillies clinched the National League East pennant for the Expos. It was the team's first championship since their creation in 1969.

This set the stage for the 1981 National League Championship Series (NLCS) against the National League West champions, the Los Angeles

Dodgers. Rogers pitched Game 3 and was no less impressive than his previous starts during the second half of the season. He pitched a complete game, beating the Dodgers by a score of 4–1 and giving the Expos a 2–1 lead in the series.

The NLCS then moved to Montreal where the Dodgers won Game 4 and had the best-of-five game series deadlocked at 2–2. The fifth and deciding game was scheduled for Sunday, October 18, but was postponed due to rain. During the rain delay, Expos outfielder Terry Francona entertained the diligent, rain-soaked fans at Olympic Stadium by charging out of the dugout and plunging into a pool of rainwater that accumulated in shallow right field.

The following day, Monday, October 19, weather conditions were no better: cloudy, 50 kilometre winds and a temperature of only 4 degrees Celsius. Yet the rescheduled Game 5 proceeded.

In front of over 36,000 fans, Expos starter Ray Burris pitched an exceptional game, giving up only one run and five hits. His opponent, future 1981 National League Rookie of the Year Fernando Valenzuela, also gave up only one run. But by the eighth inning, Burris was beginning to tire. Rogers, who had been warming up in the Expos' bullpen since the fifth inning, told manager Jim Fanning and pitching coach Galen Cisco that he would be available to relieve Burris if needed. Both agreed and Rogers was put in as a relief pitcher in the top of the ninth inning. He faced Rick Monday and, at 4:10 p.m., the Expos' hopes of appearing in a World Series for the first time ended as Rogers pitched a sinker, which Monday hit out of the park for a solo home run that gave the Dodgers a 2–1 lead.

The game ended in the bottom of the ninth with two Expos on base when Jerry White hit a grounder to second baseman Davey Lopes, who threw to first base and got the third out. The Los Angeles Dodgers won the National League pennant. This sad day in the Expos' history was later dubbed by *The Gazette* as Dodger Blue Monday, which was later shortened to Blue Monday.

Rogers, although disappointed by the result of his pitch, still saw the situation in a philosophical manner. "This one game will be a little harder to forget than the performances of the past month will be to remember. But if that's not human nature, I've missed the beat somewhere," he said.

The Dodgers went on to beat the Yankees in the 1981 World Series. Although fans still never forgot Blue Monday, they also never forgot the exciting season that the Expos had given them.

**Which father of a former Canadian Prime Minister was a key investor in the Montreal Royals during the early 1930s?**

➥**Jean-Charles Emile (Charlie) Trudeau**, father of Pierre Elliott Trudeau, was a Montreal businessman who became a millionaire when he sold his chain of service stations to Imperial Oil.

In 1933, Trudeau became the key investor of the Montreal Royals at a time when the club was on the verge of financial collapse, owing $51,000 in back taxes to the city and to the mortgage company that owned Delorimier Stadium, the Royals' home turf. Trudeau reluctantly chose to invest $25,000 in the team, writing "in protest" on the back of the cheque (although he was secretly an avid sports enthusiast and enjoyed owning a baseball club). In the long run, his cheque helped the team's fortune. That year, lights were installed at Delorimier Stadium, which led to night baseball. Management also changed when Trudeau hired Hector Racine as its president. Racine, who was also the president of the company that owned and operated the Mount Royal Arena, the Canadiens' old playing ground before their move to the Forum in 1926, was instrumental to the Royals' survival. Racine had a sharp business acumen and orchestrated the deal that made the Royals the minor league AAA affiliate to the Brooklyn Dodgers in 1938 (they were previously associated with the Pittsburgh Pirates).

Described by biographer George Radwanski as "a very extrovert of a man, with dark hair, intense eyes, a thin toothbrush moustache and quick, nervous movements and speech," Charlie Trudeau was an avid sports lover. He taught his son Pierre to box, shoot a gun, make a bow and arrow, and wrestle. Summers were spent at the family's lodge in Lac Tremblant in the Laurentians, where they indulged in canoeing, swimming, running, mountain climbing, and hiking.

That year, the Royals finished the season in sixth place. Two years later, Charlie Trudeau died from pneumonia at the age of 46, following a trip to the Royals' spring training camp in Orlando, Florida. That same year, the team won the International League pennant.

# In what discontinued event did Montreal policeman Étienne Desmarteau win Canada's first Olympic gold medal at the 1904 Games in St. Louis?

→**The 56-pound paving stone throw,** which was a precursor to the hammer throw.

Desmarteau's family came from a long line of members possessing Herculean strength, several of which worked as blacksmiths in Boucherville, a suburb south of Montreal. Considering their lineage, it was only appropriate that Desmarteau, along with his brother Zachary, make the 56-pound stone throw their specialty. The Desmarteau brothers, both police officers, won countless athletic meets as representatives of the Montreal Police Athletic Association (MPAA). Étienne even won the Canadian championships in 1902, 1903 and 1904, and held two world records.

The first female Canadian athletes to win gold medals at the Olympics were Fannie Rosenfeld, Florence Bell, Ethel Smith, and Montrealer Myrtle Cook, all members of the women's 400 metre relay team. They won gold at the 1928 Games in Amsterdam, the first Olympics where women athletes were allowed to compete in the track and field events. Cook went on to become a sports columnist for *The Montreal Star*.

When the 31-year-old Desmarteau announced his desire to compete in the 1904 Olympic Games in St. Louis, he met resistance. Not only did the Montreal Police Department not want to give him time off work for what they deemed to be a frivolous pastime, but the MPAA refused to sponsor his trip. It took the help of Desmarteau's immediate supervisor, who recommended that he be allowed to go, to convince the MPAA to underwrite part of the trip to the Olympics.

Desmarteau competed in the 56-pound paving stone throw against his long-time chief rival, John Flanagan, a New York City policeman who held the current world record.

It was a stifling hot and humid day when the two policemen faced off for the gold medal. Flanagan was mildly ill due to the unrelenting St. Louis heat but Desmarteau was in fine form. Using a personal method of making one turn before throwing the stone, Desmarteau's best throw landed at 34 feet 4 inches. Flanagan's best throw fell a foot short. The gold went to Desmarteau. His jubilant American rival cheered him on as members of the American track and field team hoisted him on their shoulders and carried him around the stadium grounds. Back in Montreal, he was greeted as a hero.

Étienne Desmarteau died of typhoid fever in 1905. The 56-pound paving stone throw, the event that won him Canada's first Olympic gold medal, was discontinued after the 1904 Games. It was revived for the 1920 Games in Antwerp but was dropped for good afterwards.

Desmarteau's contribution to Canadian Olympic history was all but forgotten until 1955, when he was posthumously inducted into Canada's Sports Hall of Fame. Twenty-one years later, his legacy was preserved when one of the venues for the 1976 Montreal Olympics was named in his honour.

**In 1958, the fight for the World Light Heavyweight title in boxing was held at the Montreal Forum and was one of the few major title matches to be held in Montreal. Who were the two challengers?**

➥**Yvon Durrelle and Archie Moore.** On December 10, 1958, Yvon (The Flying Fisherman) Durrelle, a native of New Brunswick and the Canadian and British Empire Light Heavyweight Champion, faced veteran American boxer and defending champion Archie Moore for the World Light Heavyweight title. The event was the first world title fight to be televised in the United States while taking place in another country.

Promoter Eddie Quinn anticipated an attendance of 15,000 fans for the 15-round match, and expected to collect $100,000 from admissions and $75,000 from television broadcasting rights (the fight was aired on ABC in the US and the CBC across Canada). However, when a decision was made to black out the fight in Quebec, ticket sales increased to $125,000, a record for an indoor boxing match in Canada. Moore's cut was a guaranteed 40 percent while Durrelle received $12,000 and 20 percent.

Excitement was high for the fight. Over 800 people showed up at the St. Jean Baptiste Gym to see Durrelle and Moore do their respective workouts. Durrelle trimmed down from 201 pounds to 174 pounds while Moore pared himself down from 218 pounds to 173 pounds and claimed he was in the best shape of his career, although he spent most of his training time trying to shrug off a mild head cold.

Both combatants went into the fight with different strategies. Durrelle said he had only one way of fighting: "Keep walking in and throwing — until one of us gets down". Moore, although not wanting to predict a knockout decision, was hoping that he would score one so that he could establish an all-time record of 127 knockouts in his career.

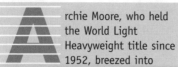

rchie Moore, who held the World Light Heavyweight title since 1952, breezed into Montreal on December 4, arrogantly declaring that he was the Canadian heavyweight boxing champion. "Say I beat [James J.] Parker [of Edmonton] didn't I? I guess that makes me Canadian champion," he told *The Montreal Star*. Yvon Durrelle couldn't wait for the match on December 10 at the Forum to prove him wrong.

Montreal Star sports reporter Red Fisher was a little more blunt and direct about how he saw the outcome of the fight: "I'm hoping that Durrelle knocks his block off."

On December 10, 8,848 people saw Archie Moore defeat Durrelle by a knockout at the 49 second mark of the 11th round. Moore almost lost the fight in the fifth round when Durrelle's hard right punch left him crumpled and dazed on the canvas. But he had enough strength to get up at the six count. After the fight, Moore said Durrelle was one of the strongest fighters he had ever faced next to Rocky Marciano. On the other hand, Durrelle broke down and cried after the match and told The Star: "I think that I have let down the people in the Maritimes. Now I'm going home to fish and I have no other bouts planned." The fight was voted as the sports story of the year by the Canadian Press.

A rematch was held the following year in which Durrelle lost to Moore by a knockout in the third round.

Durrelle retired from boxing in 1961 and pursued a career in wrestling, only to return to boxing for a brief comeback in 1963, before finally retiring from the ring in 1967. He is a member of the New Brunswick Sports Hall of Fame, Canada's Sports Hall of Fame, and the Canadian Boxing Hall of Fame.

**In the spring of 1946, the Montreal Royals broke a fundamental barrier in the world of baseball. Which barrier did they break?**

➥**The colour barrier** when Jackie Robinson, a sharecropper's son from Cairo, Georgia, made his debut for the Brooklyn Dodgers' AAA farm club.

When Jackie Robinson went on to make his professional baseball debut as a member of the Montreal Royals on April 19, 1946, Montreal Daily Star sports columnist Baz O'Meara heralded the event as "another emancipation day for the Negro race. A day that Abe Lincoln would like. Because today Jackie Robinson, first colored ballplayer to step forth in a regularly scheduled game in organized parks, gets his big chance." Next to O'Meara's column was a large photo of Lincoln, surrounded by Brooklyn Dodgers president/owner Branch Rickey, Royals president Hector Racine, Royals manager Clay Hopper and Robinson.

Not many fans and southern-born ballplayers shared O'Meara's enthusiasm for Robinson's colour barrier-breaking debut. One of them was Clay Hopper, who was appointed as the Royals' manager that same year. Born in Mississippi and a worker in the cotton industry during off-season, Hopper worked alongside Rickey first in the St. Louis Cardinals, then the Brooklyn Dodgers organization.

True to his southern roots, Hopper was adamantly opposed to integration, especially in baseball, and had asked Rickey not to have him manage a club with a Black player. During spring training, when the two men saw Robinson perform a tricky play on the field, Rickey turned to Hopper and told him he thought Robinson was "superhuman". Hopper replied, "Do you think a nigger's a human being?" Hopper's question infuriated Rickey and Hopper was told that he had no choice but to accept that Robinson was a member of the team. Rickey also insisted that Hopper soften his public stance on integration so that Robinson would see no obvious signs of his opposition to integration.

Hopper's opinion of Robinson and his abilities changed during the course of spring training when he saw Robinson's determination and skill.

Robinson played his first game for the Royals at their season opener at Roosevelt Field against the Jersey City Giants. Robinson chose to combat the prejudice, bigotry, threats and ignorance that he was facing on and off the field by showing the crowd his skill. He went 4 for 5, with two singles, a sprint bunt, two stolen bases, two runs batted in (RBIs), and a three-run homer. The Royals easily beat the Giants by a score of 14–1. The fans in Jersey City instantly warmed up to Robinson as they besieged and swarmed him in the Royals' dugout with warm wishes.

This was the start of a very successful season for Robinson and the Royals, which was capped off by their victory in the International League's Little World Series over Louisville. After the deciding game of the Series at Delorimier Stadium, in which Robinson was paraded around the field on the shoulders of the fans, Hopper met with Robinson in the Royals' clubhouse and told him: "You're a great ballplayer and a fine gentleman. It's been wonderful having you on the team." When Robinson left the clubhouse, he was mobbed by more fans who wanted to touch him and shouted: "Il a gagné ses épaulettes" — "He earned his stripes," and then almost ripped his clothes off, which prompted Robinson to run away from the adoring mob.

Sam Maltin, a sports reporter for *The Montreal Herald* and a close friend of Robinson, remarked: "It was probably the only day in history that a black man ran from a white mob with love instead of lynching on its mind."

Jackie Robinson went on to join the Brooklyn Dodgers in 1947 where he won the National League Rookie of the Year Award and carved out his 10-year Hall of Fame career.

**In the 1953 Stanley Cup final, Elmer Lach scored the winning goal against the Boston Bruins, giving the Canadiens their seventh championship. The moment is captured on film in a famous photo showing Lach and Maurice Richard in an airborne victory embrace. But what happened to Lach as photographer Roger St-Jean captured this championship moment?**

➥**He broke his nose.** The excitement broke out when, at the 1:22 overtime mark of Game 5 at the Forum, Maurice Richard passed the puck to Lach from behind the Bruins' net and proceeded to flip a waist-high backhand shot past goalie Jim Henry. The Canadiens won the game 1–0 and their first Stanley Cup since 1945–1946.

Richard and Lach celebrated the winning goal with a mid-air embrace. However, Richard let the excitement get the best of him. He hugged Lach with such force that he accidentally broke his nose (although Lach later admitted that he didn't feel a thing at the moment of impact).

The moment of the Lach-Richard collision was captured by photographer Roger St-Jean. Also shown in the picture, on the left-hand side, was Boston Bruins forward and friend of Lach Milt Schmidt, seated on the Forum ice with a dejected look on his face.

Lach, who retired after the 1952–1953 season, said in Dick Irvin's book *The Habs* that his 1953 Cup-winning goal was a rather simple one. "It was one of those plays that happens so fast you just do it, without thinking too much about it. You don't take the time to think."

*Elmer Lach (left) and Maurice Richard in an airborne embrace after Lach's Stanley Cup-winning goal for the Montreal Canadiens in 1953. Boston Bruins Milt Schmidt (far left) sits on the ice in disbelief.*

On the other hand, Schmidt took that moment (and his rather inauspicious way of getting immortalized in Roger St-Jean's photo) more harshly than Lach. A year later, in 1954, Schmidt saw the photo in question hanging on the wall of the Montreal Press Club at the Mount Royal Hotel. Letting his frustration get the best of him, Schmidt then told the bartender: "If that thing is still there next year, I'll throw a bottle of beer at it." He then stormed out of the Press Club and never returned. He also received a jigsaw puzzle version of the picture, which he threw into the fireplace. Years later, he regretted his heat-of-the-moment act. "Maybe I should have kept it. Might be worth a lot of money today."

**On July 17, 1976, the opening ceremonies of the Summer Olympics took place in Montreal. During the ceremonies, Stéphane Préfontaine and Sandra Henderson accomplished what Olympic first?**

→ **It was the first time that two people shared the honour of lighting the Olympic flame.** The pair was selected after an extensive search in Ontario and Quebec for two people who would best represent the two host provinces of the 1976 Olympics as well as "bring a message of hope to all the young athletes of the world".

Henderson, 16, was a native of Toronto and was a third-place finisher at the 1975 Canadian Junior Gymnastics Finals. She had competed in Israel, Germany and the United Kingdom, and hoped to compete in the 1978 Commonwealth Games in Edmonton and in the 1980 Olympics in

Moscow. Préfontaine, 15, was from Montreal and was a student at Brébeuf College. He was a junior provincial champion in the 400 metre run.

Préfontaine and Henderson were chosen to light the torch on the evening of July 16, 1976, the day before the opening ceremonies (and following a week of practice runs with the torch, not aware of whether or not they would be chosen to bring the flame into the stadium).

That evening, around 10:15 p.m., an emotional mayor Jean Drapeau had received the flame atop Mount Royal from Kathy Kreiner, winner of a Canadian gold medal in downhill skiing at the 1976 Winter Olympics in Innsbruck, Austria. This ended a long journey for the flame, which had begun in Athens, Greece.

n a 1986 interview with *The Gazette*, Stéphane Préfontaine said this about the pressure of being one of the torch bearers: "I was so nervous, concentrating so hard not to fumble the torch or trip and fall that I forgot where I was."

The following afternoon, on July 17, after Queen Elizabeth II officially opened the Games at 4:31 p.m., Préfontaine and Henderson ran into the Olympic Stadium before a crowd of over 73,000 spectators and 7,300 athletes. Préfontaine held the lit torch above his head while Henderson ran beside him, her hand clutching his upper arm. They then climbed up to the platform containing the urn for the flame, presented the torch to the north, south, east and west, and lit the urn to symbolically start the Games.

Many of the spectators and Olympic personnel were charmed by the teenage torchbearers and thought they would make an ideal couple. In fact, two hours after the opening ceremonies, Préfontaine and Henderson were seen together holding hands. According to one Olympic official: "They seem to have an affinity for each other. They've been more or less living together for a week — except at night, of course. Hell, I hope they get married. They're tremendous kids."

But this would not occur. After the whirlwind of interviews, photo opportunities, functions, and visits with dignitaries during the balance of the Olympics, Préfontaine and Henderson went their separate ways. They made one final appearance together at the 1980 Olympics in Moscow, in which they presented the Olympic flag to its mayor as the official representatives of mayor Drapeau.

Sandra Henderson failed to make the Canadian Olympic gymnastics team in 1976 but went on to coach gymnastics at the University of Toronto. She also worked as a nurse in a Toronto hospital's cardiac unit.

*The cover of the souvenir program for the opening ceremonies of the 1976 Summer Olympics.*

She is currently married and has two children. Préfontaine gave up track and field after suffering a groin injury in 1977. He obtained a master's degree in law at Columbia University and a doctorate in political science in Paris. He remains single and is currently working as an investment banker. He was last seen in July 2001 at a ceremony commemorating the 25th anniversary of the Montreal Olympics.

**March 17, 1955 was a black day in the history of the Montreal Canadiens. The infamous Richard Riot erupted when Maurice Richard was suspended for the remainder of the 1954–1955 season as well as the playoffs. Why was Richard suspended?**

➥ He hit Boston Bruins defenceman Hal Laycoe and NHL linesman Cliff Thompson.

The incident occurred on March 13, 1955, when the Canadiens broke their 11-game unbeaten streak by losing 4–2 against the Boston Bruins at the Boston Gardens. With five minutes left in the game, Richard got into a jam with Bruins' defenceman Hal Laycoe. With a swing of his stick, Richard gave Laycoe a gash in the face. Laycoe retaliated and was sent to the penalty box for highsticking Richard (holding his stick above shoulder level while approaching him). The situation got out of control when

Richard rushed to him and continued swinging at him. Linesman Cliff Thompson had to jump between them and break the fight, but was himself punched in the face by Richard.

Still blinded by anger, Richard picked up his stick and went after Laycoe again, striking him in the head, gashing him above one eye and below the other. Richard himself was bleeding from one of Laycoe's hits and needed five stitches. Laycoe got a major penalty for drawing blood and a 10-minute misconduct penalty, and Richard got a match penalty, a $100 fine, a suspension, and a hearing with NHL president Clarence Campbell.

Prior to the 1955 Richard Riot, Maurice Richard had a number of fines imposed upon him for unsportsmanlike behaviour on and off the ice. During his 18-year career, Richard paid over $2,500 in fines to the NHL, and at the time of the Laycoe-Thompson incident, was under a $1,000 good behavior bond to the league, which prevented him from writing or uttering derogatory statements about the NHL and its officials. This resulted from a newspaper column that Richard wrote during the 1953-1954 season that attacked Campbell over a suspension imposed on teammate Bernie Geoffrion.

The repercussions of the confrontation were harsh for Richard. Physically, he was suffering from headaches, stomach pains, was having difficulty sleeping, and was sent to the Montreal General Hospital for his nervous condition.

Richard had to leave his hospital bed to attend his hearing, which took place at Campbell's office with coach Dick Irvin and Ken Reardon, who was representing general manager Frank Selke. The meeting lasted two-and-a-half hours and was the longest hearing ever held in the NHL's history to discuss a single incident involving a player.

On March 16, it was announced that Maurice Richard would be suspended not only for the remainder of the season but the playoffs as well. Hal Laycoe was cleared of all charges.

Richard's teammates and fans were infuriated. Habs defenceman Doug Harvey told *The Montreal Star* that Campbell had put too much weight on Thompson's testimony. "If I was bleeding from the head like the Rocket was and somebody jumped on me like that, I would have hit him too," he said. Veteran NHL referee Frank Udvari had his reservations about Thompson, who was a rookie linesman, and admitted that he had made a couple of other bad calls during that game. The Forum, the NHL, and a variety of Montreal newspapers and radio stations received a flood of calls from angry fans, many of whom were sobbing women or were so furious that they could hardly talk.

Mayor Jean Drapeau agreed that Richard deserved to be punished but thought it was wrong to punish the team, whose chances of winning first place in the NHL were now greatly diminished.

By March 17, the fans' anger reached a high pitch as the Habs were slated to play the Detroit Red Wings at the Forum. Campbell, in a rather brave gesture, attended the game. During the first period, Campbell was slapped in the face by a fan who had originally extended his hand out for a handshake. Shortly after, a tear gas canister exploded inside the Forum. A riot erupted and resulted in the arrest of 41 people. The Forum suffered $25,000 in damages and a path of looting and destruction along St-Catherine Street affected 50 stores and cost the city over $100,000.

The incident, later known as the Richard Riot, was deemed by The Star as "a black eye for Montreal".

# OH, WHAT A SIGHT TO SEE!

## montreal immortalized in stone, brick and steel

**Which English governess, who inspired a popular Broadway musical, spent her final years in Montreal, and is buried in Mount Royal Cemetery?**

➥**Anna Leonowens.** The wife of an officer in the British India Service, Leonowens travelled to Thailand after her husband's death in 1859 to become the governess of King Mongkut of Siam's 64 children, which she served from 1862 to 1867. She chronicled her years in King Mongkut's court in her book *An English Governess at the Court of Siam,* which inspired the 1946 movie *Anna and the King of Siam,* and the hit Broadway musical *The King and I.*

Leonowens' post-Siam years were dedicated to the education of children, first in London, then New York City, then Halifax. In 1897, 30 years after she left Siam, Anna went to live in Montreal with her daughter and son-in-law, who was the general manager of the Merchants Bank of Canada.

Residing on McTavish Street, Anna led an active life in Montreal. She lectured to various societies and charities on Chinese, Indian and Egyptian cultures, and spent countless hours in the reading room of the Redpath Library, engrossed in its large collection of books dealing with China. She also became involved with the Baby Foundling Hospital, in which she served as president. During that time, she managed to convince the Roman Catholic Church to modify their practice of hurriedly baptizing newborn babies out of fear that exposing them to the cold air would lead to pneumonia and other fatal ailments.

In her last years, she took care of her son-in-law after he suffered a paralyzing stroke. On January 19, 1915, Anna Leonowens died following a stroke at the age of 84. She is buried in Mount Royal Cemetery next to her daughter and son-in-law.

**Before the death of Montreal mayor Camillien Houde in September of 1958, his crypt at Cote des Neiges Cemetery was made to his specifications, and was modelled after the tomb of what 19th century military leader?**

→**Napoleon Bonaparte.** Houde, who served as Montreal's mayor for 18 years off and on between 1928 and 1954, died in his sleep on September 11, 1958, at the age of 69. The rotund, jovial figure that ruled Montreal with flair and controversy stepped down in 1954 due to ill health. For the last four years of his life, Houde lived a quiet, secluded existence and made his last public appearance at a rally for Quebec Premier Maurice Duplessis in June of 1956. He died suddenly of undisclosed causes after spending an evening with his family.

Mayor Sarto Fournier, when he learned of Houde's death, declared that a civic funeral would be held in his honour, and that the city would have a half-day civic holiday on September 15 for the funeral. Houde's body lay in state in the Hall of Honour of Montreal City Hall where over 150,000 Montrealers filed past the open casket to pay their last respects to a man they called Mr. Montreal. The funeral at Notre-Dame Basilica also attracted many major political figures.

*Mayor Camillien Houde's tomb, inspired by Napoleon Bonaparte's tomb in Paris.*

He was buried at Cote des Neiges Cemetery in a tomb that Houde had designed and built himself in 1955. It was based on Napoleon Bonaparte's tomb at the Hôtel des Invalides in Paris, and displayed two flights of steps that lead to a recess where indirect lighting fell at nighttime. The left side of the structure had the City of Montreal's coat of arms and alongside it was a cross and olive branch. The tombstone displayed Houde's full name, birth and death dates, and offered a chronological resume of his political career.

But why had Houde selected Napoleon as his source of inspiration? Because Napoleon was "the complete master of modern politics," said Houde in a newspaper interview prior to his death.

**What Montreal Canadiens superstar of the 1920s and 1930s had his funeral held at the Montreal Forum in front of thousands of fans, and is buried in Mount Royal Cemetery?**

**Howie Morenz.** Known as the Stratford Streak, the Mitchell Meteor and the Babe Ruth of Hockey, Morenz was the fastest skater of his generation, and was a symbol of the Montreal Canadiens' first dynasty in the late 1920s and early 1930s.

Morenz was born in Mitchell, Ontario, in 1902 and had a calling for hockey. His speedy skating style made him one of the most popular players in Ontario, first in his hometown of Mitchell, and later in Stratford, where he played in a junior league. Morenz signed with the Canadiens in the summer of 1922 for $1,600 and first played for the team the following year. During his first 11 years with the Habs, Morenz won two scoring championships, three Hart Trophies as the NHL's most valuable player, and three Stanley Cups (in 1924, 1930, and 1931).

It was during a game against Chicago at the Forum on January 28, 1937, that Morenz crashed into the boards. The tip of his skate got caught in the hardwood board and, as he fell, the weight of his body cracked his leg. Morenz was taken off the ice on a stretcher and brought to St. Luc Hospital on Dorchester Street. During his convalescence, Morenz wondered if he would ever skate again. However, with assurance from the team doctor and his friends that he would be fine, Morenz was reassured. He told teammate Aurèle Joliat, during a visit to the hospital: "I'll be all right. I'll be up there watching you in the playoffs."

On the evening of March 8, Morenz got out of his bed and, as his feet reached the floor, crumpled to the floor and died of a heart attack just as his wife and Canadiens coach Cecil Hart were about to enter his room. Morenz was 35 years old.

His sudden death stunned hockey fans across North America and deeply affected his teammates. Three days later, on March 11, a funeral service was held, not in a church, but in the place that made him famous . . . the Montreal Forum. Thousands of fans packed the Forum to pay their last respects. Morenz's coffin was placed on centre ice and was surrounded by an honour guard of his Canadiens teammates: Aurèle Joliat, Johnny Gagnon, Pit Lépine, and Armand Mondou. Numerous NHL officials and players were also in attendance.

On May 3, 1952, 15 years after Howie Morenz's death, his daughter Marlene, an accomplished figure skater, maintained the family ties with the Montreal Canadiens when she married Habs superstar Bernie Geoffrion.

The coffin was surrounded by 150 floral tributes, including a number 7 (Morenz's sweater number) made of lilies and red roses from Aurèle Joliat, and a bouquet of flowers with a card saying "To our daddy" placed in Morenz's hands by his widow and three children.

After the funeral, Morenz's body was taken to Mount Royal Cemetery for burial. As his body was being lowered, Montreal Maroons player King Clancy whispered in an emotion-choked voice to his teammate Alex Connell that Morenz was "the greatest of them all". Connell nodded in agreement.

One of Montreal's most colourful characters during the 19th century was a former British Army quartermaster named Charles McKiernan, who was best known for running a tavern near Montreal's waterfront, and for his charitable nature toward the city's poor and indigent. What was McKiernan's rather meaty nickname, immortalized on his tombstone at Mount Royal Cemetery?

→Joe Beef. McKiernan got the nickname from his British Army comrades during the Crimean War (1854–1856) because he always succeeded in finding food and provisions for the troops of his regiment. After the war, Joe Beef moved to Montreal where he served at the British Garrison on Ile Ste. Helene.

After leaving the army, Joe opened his famous tavern on the corner of de la Commune and Callières streets near the waterfront. His clientele was composed of an odd mix of sailors, city drifters, poors, toughs, and criminals who saw the tavern as a refuge. Most came for Joe Beef's hearty meal, made up of plenty of soup and bread, and costing only 10 cents. Those who could not afford the meal received it free of charge. In addition to regular servings of beer and liquor, Beef served an average of 600 meals per day.

Joe Beef's tavern also doubled as a homeless shelter where every night, 100 people were accommodated on wooden and iron bunk beds located on the second floor. Again, the cost for a night's lodging was 10 cents but those who could not afford the fee were admitted for free but had to meet Beef's strict standards: those who showed up dirty and unshaven were given a bath, were shaven, and were disinfected before being sent up to the second floor.

The following is an excerpt from Joe Beef's poem, which was inscribed on his tombstone at Mount Royal Cemetery: "Full many a man of wealth and power
And died and gone before
Who scorned to give a poor man bread
When he stood at his door.
But Joe took in the great unwashed,
Who shared his humble fare,
He made their life a merry one
Without a thought of care.
Their eyes are dim for loss of him
Their grief is quite sincere,
He housed them from the winter blast
And filled them with good cheer.
And when the day of reckoning comes
As come it does to all,
Such sincere mourners they'll not have
Behind their funeral-pall."

Besides the tavern, Joe Beef became reputable due to his acts of charity. During a strike by labourers at the Lachine Canal, Beef donated 3,000 loaves of bread and 500 gallons of soup to the striking workers and their families. He also kept two metal boxes on his tavern counter in which one was for cash donations to benefit the Montreal General Hospital and the other, the Notre-Dame Hospital.

Although he became a legendary figure among Montreal's poor, working class, and maritime workers, he was also greatly criticized by Montreal's press for attracting such seedy characters to his establishment. In response to the attacks, Beef distributed handbills with his picture on it that read "He cares not for Pope, Priest, Parson . . . for of Churches, Chapels, Ranters, Preachers, Beechers and such stuff Montreal has already got enough . . ."

When Joe Beef died suddenly of a heart ailment in 1889, at the age of 54, he was granted one of the biggest funerals Montreal had ever seen. The procession stretched along the length of the waterfront and included representatives of Montreal's 50 labour unions and many of the poor and homeless whom Joe Beef had aided. His large granite tombstone at Mount Royal Cemetery contained a poetic inscription that Beef wrote himself, which took aim at the city's upper class that criticized him for his charity work. Joe Beef bequeathed the premises of his tavern to the Salvation Army. In the 1980s, Montreal playwright David Fennario wrote a play called "Joe Beef" that kept alive the legend of the generous British Army quartermaster and his famous tavern, which was presented near its original site.

## Which US Civil War General became a devoutly religious, Sabbath-observing man after watching British troops drill at the Champ de Mars?

→Thomas Jonathan (Stonewall) Jackson. In 1853, Jackson, then a Major teaching artillery at the Virginia Military Institute, was in Montreal on his honeymoon. A professional soldier, Jackson was determined to go see a British military regiment on disciplined display and so, went to the Champ de Mars, a popular public drilling ground and watched the proceedings. However, Jackson's wife Eleanor, a very religious woman, frowned on the fact that the activity took place on a Sunday and disapproved of her husband's outing on this religious day.

When he returned, Eleanor reprimanded Jackson for desecrating the Sabbath. He insisted that he did no wrong, however, later had second thoughts about his deed. After further consideration back in Virginia, Jackson decided to become a devout observer of the Sabbath.

For the rest of his life, Jackson never travelled on a Sunday, never mailed a letter on a Sunday, and during the Civil War, did everything possible to prevent his troops from fighting on a Sunday.

Stonewall Jackson died from wounds sustained from friendly fire during the Battle of Chancellorsville on May 10, 1863 . . . on a Sunday!

## What was the original name of the Jacques Cartier Bridge?

↪ **The Montreal Harbor Bridge.** In the early 1920s, Montreal was experiencing an increase in motor vehicle traffic, a growth in industrialization in the east end of the city, and an expansion of suburbs on the south shore. A vital, sturdy suspension bridge link was required as the 60-year-old Victoria Bridge was no longer sufficient to meet the needs of the growing number of Montrealers crossing the St. Lawrence by automobile.

In August of 1922, the Privy Council allocated $50,000 to the Montreal Harbor Commission to conduct studies, surveys, and to come up with designs for a bridge linking the south shore to the Montreal island, all of which would be presented in Ottawa. On January 28, 1925, the Harbor Commission, after 14 meetings, selected the Delorimier Street area, at the junction of Notre-Dame and Craig streets, as the Montreal entry point for the bridge. Labelled the Montreal Harbor Bridge, it would span over the St. Lawrence River, the west point of Ile Ronde, the east point of Ile Ste. Helene, and end between Saint-Lambert and Longueuil.

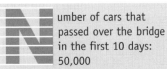

umber of cars that passed over the bridge in the first 10 days: 50,000

» Amount in tolls collected during those 10 days: $20,000
» Toll rates to cross the bridge in 1930: Five cents for pedestrians and automobile passengers, 25 cents for automobiles, 15 cents for motorcycles, and free for children five years of age and under
» Maximum speed limit for all vehicles crossing the bridge: 25 miles per hour.

Construction began in October of 1925 and the bridge opened on May 16, 1930, six months ahead of schedule. It featured four traffic lanes (two for cars, two for tramways), sidewalks on both sides, and was a success from the beginning.

The official opening took place on May 24 and was attended by politicians, judges, clergymen, and members of the Harbor Commission. Prime Minister Mackenzie King officially opened the bridge by telephone from his office in Ottawa as he could not attend the ceremonies (he was about to dissolve Parliament and call a general election). In his address to the crowd, King said that the Montreal Harbor Bridge "will stand in the eyes of the world as one of the greatest engineering achievements of our age, a monument to the genius and skill of the Canadian people."

In 1934, the Montreal Harbor Commission changed the name of the bridge to the Jacques Cartier Bridge, in commemoration of the 400th anniversary of Cartier's first voyage to Quebec.

What Montreal church served as the headquarters of the Montreal Catholic Archdiocese and was built as a quarter-scale replica of St. Peter's Basilica in Rome?

➡**Mary Queen of the World Cathedral,** which was originally known as St. James the Greater. The church was initially located on the corner of St-Denis and St-Catherine streets but was destroyed by fire in 1852. Ignace Bourget, the spiritual leader of Montreal's Catholic Archdiocese, decided to rebuild the cathedral but on Dorchester Street, in the heart of Montreal's English-speaking Protestant neighbourhood.

His fellow clergymen thought Bourget was mad to build a Catholic cathedral in a Protestant area. However, Bourget based his decision on his right to assert the Catholic Church's authority in the city, and cited his intense loyalty to the Vatican and Pope Pius IX in a city that was ruled by the British.

To further illustrate his loyalty to Rome, it was decided that the new cathedral would be based on the Vatican's nerve centre, the neo-baroque St. Peter's Basilica in Rome. Virtually all details mirrored St. Peter's, even the religious statues that graced its roof. In the Montreal version, however, the statues did not represent the 12 Apostles of Christ, but the Montreal parishes that contributed financially to the construction of the cathedral.

Besides housing the Montreal Archdiocese, Mary Queen of the World Cathedral now serves as the final resting place of all Montreal Catholic bishops and archbishops, who are interred in the mortuary chapel located in the east side of the cathedral.

In September of 1962, which Montreal building, designed by New York architect William Zeckendorf (who was also the architect of the United Nations building), became the first modern office building to open in the city?

➡**Place Ville-Marie.** The idea for Place Ville-Marie came as early as 1955 when Canadian National Railway (CNR) president Donald Gordon was revitalizing the downtown core and developed a new Central Station and the Queen Elizabeth Hotel to fill the 22-acre gaping hole containing the CNR tracks, which was regarded as an eyesore.

*Place Ville-Marie, Montreal's first modern office building, nearing completion in 1962.*

New York-based architect William Zeckendorf proposed a major office building to fill four acres, which would mean, according to Gordon's biographer Joseph Schull, "potential for a new center of gravity and a fresh start for the city." He even told Gordon that his firm would absorb the cost of constructing a plan and model for the office complex, and that Gordon and the CNR were under no obligation to accept Zeckendorf's plan.

Zeckendorf presented the proposed office complex to Gordon in the spring of 1956 and suggested that it become a city within a city. According to Zeckendorf's plan, this new complex ". . . will bear the proud name of Ville Marie, a name given . . . in 1642 to the first European settlement on the island . . ." He continued by saying: "The most striking element of the Ville Marie plan is the metal and glass tower — a cruciform skyscraper 550 feet in height with forty floors of office space . . . This structure, the tallest and largest in Canada, is designed to house major corporations, four of which will be provided with their own separate ground floor lobbies."

The plan for Place Ville-Marie was not approved immediately; it would take 11 more months of studies by the CNR and the federal government before it received the much-needed approval, which was obtained in early 1958. Io Ming Pei, the prominent Chinese-born architect, was appointed to oversee the building's design.

**B**esides the 42-storey office tower, Place Ville-Marie also contained an underground promenade with 50 stores and shops, two cinemas, seven restaurants, and several service centres, making it Montreal's first enclosed, air-conditioned, and heated shopping mall. The cost to build Place Ville-Marie was $80 million, but was inflated to $105 million when the cost of building the shopping complex and underground parking garage was factored in.

Zeckendorf appointed all the major players in the construction of Place Ville-Marie. However, Zeckendorf faced major opposition by members of Montreal's conservative business establishment, especially because part of the construction plan for Place Ville-Marie was to demolish the St. James Club on Dorchester Street, their venerable, exclusive meeting place. One of its fiercest opponents was Royal Bank president James Muir. In a heated exchange between the two, Zeckendorf proposed that the Royal Bank move its headquarters from St. James Street to Place Ville-Marie, and proposed that the 42-storey cruciform tower be named after the bank. "You'll be king of the hill — the business will come to you," Zeckendorf told Muir, as a way to encourage him to make the move. When Muir rejected the idea, Zeckendorf suggested that he could buy the Royal Bank himself, and then told the flustered bank president to think about his idea.

After five weeks of mulling it over, Muir agreed to establish the Royal Bank's new headquarters at Place Ville-Marie. Shortly afterwards, other major and minor Canadian corporations followed the Royal Bank to Place Ville-Marie, including Trans-Canada Airlines (later Air Canada), Montreal Trust and the Aluminum Company of Canada (Alcan).

On September 13, 1962, Place Ville-Marie officially opened in an elaborate ceremony attended by 1,500 dignitaries, including Gordon, Zeckendorf, mayor Jean Drapeau, Quebec Premier Jean Lesage, and Montreal Archbishop Cardinal Paul-Émile Léger. *The Montreal Star* heralded the opening of Montreal's first modern office complex saying that "Place Ville Marie has given Montreal a new feeling of excitement. Just as it created a new focal point in the heart of Montreal, so has its dominant 42-storey structure become a new symbol of the economic vitality of Canada's largest city."

## What role did the Sun Life Building play in World War II?

→ **It stored most of Britain's wealth from 1940 to 1945.** In the spring of 1940, fearing an invasion of Britain by Nazi Germany, British Prime Minister Winston Churchill felt that the British wealth needed to be preserved to finance the war effort abroad. As a result, he shipped all of Britain's gold, all of its paper securities, and billions of dollars worth of artifacts, including the crown jewels, to Canada. The paper securities and crown jewels were secured in the third-level basement of the Sun Life Building. Here, it was held in 900 large cabinets and guarded around the clock by Royal Canadian Mounted Police officers until the war ended. The British gold was sent to Ottawa and was stored in the vaults of the Bank of Canada.

Built in stages between 1904 and 1933, the Sun Life Building was at one time known as Montreal's tallest structure and largest building in the British Empire. Others called it the Wedding Cake because the building rose in tiers of decreasing size and was supported by a number of columns, just like a wedding cake.

Besides storing Britain's wealth, the Sun Life Building also housed the exiled government of Nazi-occupied Luxembourg.

*The Sun Life Building in 1966, which not only housed the Sun Life Assurance Company and the National Hockey League, but also most of Britain's wealth during World War II.*

**On October 14, 1966, there was an air of excitement in Montreal as its subway system, known as the metro, was officially inaugurated. After which European city was Montreal's metro system based?**

→ **Paris, France.** When construction began on the metro on May 23, 1962, officials from Paris' subway system worked alongside their Montreal counterparts and offered technical assistance, especially with regard to the underground tunnel system. Montreal also mirrored the French metro cars, which used rubber tires and contained four sets of sliding doors on each car.

On October 14, 1966, when the 16.13 mile-long, 21-station metro system was officially opened, Montreal mayor Jean Drapeau presided over the opening ceremonies and was accompanied by French Minister of State Louis Joxe, who blew the whistle from the Berri-de Montigny station to signal that trains would start running from the other stations.

The idea of building a Montreal subway system started as early as 1910 when an advertisement appeared in *The Montreal Daily Star* to promote the benefits of an underground subway system. In October of 1953, the Montreal Transportation Commission (MTC) presented a proposal for such a system. Less than eight years later, the city was authorized to build the metro and, in November of 1961, the city voted to contribute $132 million dollars toward its construction, which commenced six months later.

Drapeau was proud of the newly opened metro system and made it a focal point of his re-election campaign in 1960. In an interview published in *The Montreal Star* in October of 1966, he said that the metro would bring ". . . confidence, to the people of the city and to investors everywhere. This made (the) Metro feasible. It brought industry, hotels and skyscrapers and Expo — it brought a boom the likes of which no Montrealer has ever seen . . . Our aim is to make the subway pleasant so people will love to use it."

n September 9, 1984, the metro recorded its largest single-day use ever, as over 2 million people rode the metro for Pope John Paul II's visit to Montreal.

The system was a success. On opening day, an estimated 250,000 people rode the new white and powder blue subway trains. Most used it to commute to their workplace, but some simply rode it for fun.

Since its inauguration, the metro system has expanded from 21 stations to 67. A further expansion to Laval is slated for 2006.

# tHE City That Never Sleeps, but Always Eats

## a taste of montreal's culinary and nightclub past

**What Montreal delicatessen and smoked meat emporium, which opened in 1908, is also famous for its wall of autographed photos of celebrities, all past visitors of the restaurant?**

→**Bens.** Located on the corner of De Maisonneuve and Metcalfe streets, Bens was founded by Ben Kravitz, a Lithuanian immigrant who, in 1908, founded a grocery store with his wife Fanny on St. Lawrence Boulevard. At first, the grocery store did not attract many customers, but when nearby factory girls stopped by and asked for sandwiches, Kravitz decided to make sandwiches with beef briskets that he pickled and smoked himself (which he learned from farmers from his native Lithuania).

At first, these factory girls were not impressed with the unappetizing look of the meat placed between two slices of bread; it was black and dirty looking from the smoking that Kravitz did over a hickory bark fire. After constant pleading and begging from Kravitz to try the sandwich for free, a factory girl reluctantly sampled it. She liked this exotic smoked meat sandwich and spread the word to her colleagues. Soon, business picked up.

In 1929, Ben and Fanny took a chance and opened a Bens Delicatessen Sandwich Shop in the heart of downtown Montreal, behind the old Mount Royal Hotel. This move was profitable as tourists, night owls, and visiting celebrities began to fancy a late-night stop at Bens for a smoked meat sandwich, which in 1954 cost 30 cents.

According to a 1954 article in *Maclean's,* Bens attracted 8,000 customers per day to its 150-seat deli. Although it offered a wide-ranging menu of delicatessen-style food, approximately 80 percent of Bens' clientele preferred the smoked meat sandwich, dill pickle, and coffee combo.

Some of Bens' star-studded admirers included:

» Comedian Red Skelton, who openly plugged Bens during his appearances at Montreal vaudeville houses.

» George McManus, creator of the long-running comic strip "Bringing Up Father", plugged Bens in his strip with a caption stating "You want to be strong? Eat at Bens."

» Famed 1920s and 1930s bandleader Paul Whiteman called Bens "the place where I fall off my diet".

» Members of the Metropolitan Opera Company of New York, who once performed an impromptu concert while dining at Bens.

» Former Prime Minister Pierre Trudeau, who always took his three sons to Bens.

An article published in the April 15, 1954 issue of *Maclean's* magazine cited these two examples of Bens' international reputation, and the lengths that people would go to buy them:

» A restaurant owner in Miami, Florida offered to buy Bens' smoked meat recipe on a royalty basis.

» A large sign was placed outside a restaurant in San Diego, California that said: "Bens — 3,018 miles northeast."

Bens' walls are decorated with over 200 framed autographed photos that serve as a visual record of the scores of celebrities who enjoyed those famous smoked meat sandwiches. The pictures include a wide variety of personalities from actors, singers, poets, sports figures, and even astronauts. They include television variety show host Ed Sullivan, American singer/actor Burl Ives, comedians Milton Berle and John Candy, popular 1940s and 1950s singing group the Inkspots, Canadian actor Al Waxman, legendary American vaudevillian Sophie Tucker, and Quebecois artist Jean-Paul Riopelle.

After years of working around the clock at the restaurant, Ben Kravitz died in 1956 at the age of 73. Bens is still in operation and is still located on the same corner of downtown Montreal, but in a larger building next door to the original building. Its interior has remained virtually unchanged over the past 50 years, complete with vinyl booths, yellow Formica counters, green tiled floors and neon lighting. It continues to be run by Kravitz family members and serves approximately 2 million people per year.

The restaurant pays homage to its customers with this inscription over the entrance door: "Through these doors pass the nicest people in the world . . . our customers".

## What was the name of the restaurant, located in Old Montreal during the 1930s, that displayed a floor covered in silver dollars?

➡ **The Silver Dollar Palace.** Located on the corner of Notre-Dame Street and Bonsecours Market, and facing the venerable Nelson Monument, the Silver Dollar Palace was known for its fine food, cheaply priced liquor, and its floor, inlaid with one-foot cement squares in which silver dollars were cemented. According to Montreal Herald columnist Al Palmer, a multitude of customers would try to pry the silver dollars from the floor but without success.

Silver dollars were also fastened along the restaurant's 40-foot mahogany bar, at two-foot intervals. "And almost hourly some stranger would attempt to pick one up," wrote Palmer. "No one ever tried twice because whenever one was touched the bartender would step on a switch giving the touchee a shock."

## What legendary hole-in-the-wall Montreal lunch counter opened in 1932 as a combination cigar store and barbershop?

➡ **Wilensky's or Wilensky's Light Lunch.** The eatery was founded by Harry Wilensky, the owner of a chain of barbershops in Montreal around 1910. In 1932, Wilensky opened another barbershop on the corner of Fairmount and St-Urbain streets, but this time, combined it with a cigar store. As the Depression progressed, Wilensky closed the barbershop and concentrated solely on candy, cigars, and sandwiches.

Alongside the hot dogs, soft drinks and taffy apples, Wilensky's also served deli fare, including a sandwich that would become known world-wide: a combination of grilled salami and bologna on a lightly toasted roll with some mustard. The Wilensky Special became the favourite of numerous celebrities, hockey players, business executives and nearby garment workers. In fact, during the 1970s, three buyers from Vancouver were doing business in the garment district. When they were offered by one of the clothing businesses to be taken to dinner at a prominent Montreal steakhouse, one of the buyers replied: "You trying to bribe us? Just take us to Wilensky's".

The late Mordecai Richler was a regular Wilensky's customer. In fact, as a child, his grandfather took him there every Saturday. When a film version of *The Apprenticeship of Duddy Kravitz* was made in Montreal in 1973, a scene was filmed at Wilensky's. Much to the dismay of regular customers, the lunch counter was closed for one week to shoot the scene (in which owner Moe Wilensky had a bit part as Syd).

Wilensky's moved to its current location on the corner of Fairmount and Clark streets in 1952 and took all of the old fixtures with them, including its long counter, nine bar stools, and three toasters. The Wilensky Special has become world famous, with write-ups about it in *Frommer's 2001 Travel Guide*, *National Geographic Traveler* magazine, Mordecai Richler's novel *The Apprenticeship of Duddy Kravitz*, and even in a play appropriately called *The Special*, by Montreal playwright and business columnist Mike Gutwillig.

After Harry Wilensky's death, his son Moe took over the business, followed by his own son Bernard, who ran the enterprise until his death in 2000. Bernard's brother Asher now runs the famed lunch counter with his mother Ruth.

Crowds continue to flock to Wilensky's to sample the Wilensky Special. Tips are not accepted. However, any tips left by customers are donated to the Quebec Heart and Stroke Foundation.

**What is the name of the Westmount community centre, located on Sherbrooke Street, which became famous for its Saturday night dances between 1941 and 1950?**

➥**Victoria Hall.** Indeed, over 800 people would attend every Saturday night to dance to the popular jazz and big band tunes of the day, and crowds would often line up outside Victoria Hall two hours before the doors opened.

The house band was the Johnny Holmes Orchestra. Bandleader Johnny Holmes organized every aspect of the Victoria Hall dances; he rented the hall, guaranteed the musicians' salaries out of his own pocket, handled the publicity, bought stage props, and hired work crews to set up the stage.

By 1942, the Johnny Holmes Orchestra featured two singers and 15 musicians, including a budding 17-year-old pianist named Oscar Peterson who stayed with the band until 1948. The Johnny Holmes Orchestra was one of the most popular and successful bands in Montreal.

The Saturday night dances at Victoria Hall were broadcast live on CBC Radio and as a result, the Johnny Holmes Orchestra received requests to play at dances, hotels, and clubs across the city.

scar Peterson, one of the world's most renowned jazz pianists, was born on August 15, 1925 in Montreal's St-Henri district, the son of a Canadian Pacific Railway porter and a domestic maid. He made his radio debut at the age of 15 on CKAC and five years later, made his national radio debut on the CBC's *Light Up and Listen* and *The Happy Gang*. In a career that spanned more than 60 years, and which included countless musical recordings, as well as concert, television, and radio appearances, Peterson won three Grammy Awards, holds an honourary degree from Concordia University, and is a member of the Juno Hall of Fame.

However, by the end of the 1940s, attendance at the weekly Victoria Hall dances declined as the fans grew older and settled into quieter lifestyles. In 1950, Holmes resigned as bandleader, gave up playing the trumpet, and got a job as a textile salesman. The band broke up a year later.

## What jazz club, located on Mountain Street, was the first to introduce bebop music to Montreal in the 1940s?

→The Café St. Michel. Located across the street from the legendary Rockhead's Paradise, the Café St. Michel became a mecca for jazz musicians and fans. It also featured Black entertainers, including the first all-Canadian Black chorus line in Canada. As well, the house band, Louis Metcalfe and the International Band, were one of the first racially mixed bands to play in Montreal. By 1946, the seven-man International Band was made up of Canadians of Japanese, French, American, West Indian, Swedish, and Mexican backgrounds.

Known as "Canada's greatest jazz band", Louis Metcalfe and the International Band were devoted to bebop music and introduced this

**S**ouvenir postcard advertisement for Café St. Michel from the 1940s: "Located at 770 Mountain Street just below St. Antoine. Café St. Michel is in the heart of Montreal's Harlem section and is known from coast to coast as the café famous for the finest colored shows in Montreal. There is an early show and a late show every night with continuous dancing to Louis Metcalfe, his trumpet and his orchestra."

style of jazz for the first time in Montreal on the stage of the Café St. Michel. A typical night at the club had Metcalfe's band play popular dance tunes during the first half of their set, followed with bebop music in the second half. They played three shows on Saturdays (at 9 p.m., 11 p.m., and 1:15 a.m.), followed by a 3 a.m. breakfast show (in which champagne and snacks were served), plus a Sunday afternoon jam session than ran until 7 p.m. After a two-hour nap break, the band would put on another two shows starting at 11 p.m. every Sunday night.

The late-night jam sessions attracted some of America's top jazz musicians including Duke Ellington and local star Oscar Peterson, who was a regular at the café.

During the 1960s, the Café St. Michel changed its name to the Harlem Paradise and later, to Soul City. It closed down by the end of the decade.

**What was the high-class hotel café and supper club that became a sought-out nightspot for celebrities such as Maurice Chevalier, Charles Laughton, and Marlene Dietrich?**

→**The Ritz Café.** Opened by the Ritz-Carlton's general manager Jean Contat in 1949, the Ritz Café was a converted storage area in the hotel's southwest corner of its basement floor. It was renovated to resemble a Paris bistro complete with oak panelling, mirror-covered square pillars, and small tables draped in blue and white-checkered tablecloths topped with replicas of Italian lamps. This conversion was done on the orders of François Dupré, the hotel's owner, to increase the hotel's revenue.

Every day after the afternoon high tea, the Ritz Café became the Ritz Café at Night and served drinks and dinner. Following dinner, the carpet was rolled up to reveal a dance floor and onstage, a repertoire of top acts such as singers Jane Morgan, Celeste Holm, and French singer Suly

Solidor, all accompanied by pianist Johnny Gallant (who was married to Montreal writer Mavis Gallant), and the Joseph Seitano Trio, appearing as the café's resident orchestra for 15 years.

In a short time, the Ritz Café became one of the most popular nightspots in Montreal, and it became impossible to get a table without a reservation. The café also attracted many international celebrities such as actors Charles Boyer and Charles Laughton, actress Marlene Dietrich and singer Maurice Chevalier, who saw the Ritz Café as a late-night place to dine and relax after their own performances in Montreal.

A typical advertisement for the Ritz Café at Night: "This is an ideal place to come for lunch or dinner. On 'Cook's Night Out' you will be surprised and pleased at our fast and efficient service as well as the delightful meal at a very moderate price. Lunch, 75 cents, Dinner, 85 cents."

*A newspaper advertisement for the Ritz Café (circa 1949), which was a favourite hangout for celebrities such as Charles Laughton and Marlene Dietrich.*

**What legendary St-Antoine Street jazz club was immortalized in Canadian author Morley Callaghan's novel *The Loved and the Lost?***

→**Rockhead's Paradise.** The club, which was located on St-Antoine Street in the heart of Montreal's old Black neighbourhood, was run by Rufus Nathanael Rockhead, a Jamaican-born immigrant who served in the Canadian Army during World War I and worked as a porter for the Canadian Pacific Railway for eight years. In 1927, while operating a successful shoeshine and hat-cleaning operation in Verdun, Rockhead wanted to open a nightclub and applied for a liquor licence. However, the provincial liquor commission repeatedly refused to grant him one because of his ethnic background.

The following year, when the new head of the liquor commission turned out to be a friend of Rockhead's lawyer, Rockhead got his liquor licence. He opened Rockhead's Paradise, a tavern, and added a lunch counter and a 15-room hotel above the tavern. In 1930, Rockhead abandoned the hotel and lunch counter and transformed Rockhead's Paradise into a nightclub that served wine and beer and featured a local Black jazz band.

Rockhead's Paradise hit its stride by 1939, catering to students, servicemen during World War II, and post-war nightclub goers who took advantage of Montreal's open city atmosphere and loved to dress up in their best for a night on the town. Patrons came to Rockhead's regularly to take in the large-scale glittering shows it presented, which featured some of the finest Black entertainers of the day such as Pearl Bailey, Cab Calloway, Louis Armstrong, Sarah Vaughan, and a young singer/dancer who performed with his father and uncle called Sammy Davis Jr. The club made Rufus Rockhead a wealthy man.

ockhead's Paradise became one of Montreal's two or three most popular nightclubs and was ranked in the same league as some of Harlem's legendary nightspots such as the Cotton Club. Some of its famous regular customers included humourist Stephen Leacock, boxers Sugar Ray Robinson and Joe Louis, and the different incarnations of the Harlem Globetrotters.

Novelist Morley Callaghan used Rockhead's Paradise as the inspiration for the nightclub scenes in his 1951 novel *The Loved and the Lost.* The book, which takes place in Montreal's Black community during the early 1950s, focuses on Peggy Sanderson, a young white girl opposed to racial prejudice who decides to live in the city's Black area, where she hangs out at Rockhead's (which was called Café St. Antoine).

However, in 1952, Rockhead paid the price for his club's late closing hours. The Quebec government revoked his liquor licence and seized over $10,000 worth of spirits because his establishment was serving alcohol after the curfew.

In 1961, nine years later, Rockhead got his liquor licence back (following a change in government) and in the 1960s, his club experienced an amazing revival with a new generation of customers. Well into the 1970s, Rockhead's Paradise filled its 300 seats within 20 minutes every Saturday night during the summer months (with the bar's Scotch supply cleaned out by midnight). And at the door, greeting customers and handing female patrons a fresh rose or carnation, was its flamboyant founder/owner Rufus Rockhead.

During the 1960s, Rockhead's Paradise was turned into a soul/rhythm and blues club, and then a jazz club in 1977, neither of which were as successful. The building was later abandoned. Rufus Rockhead died in 1981.

## In 1900, Hyman Seligman made a significant contribution to Montreal's gastronomic history. What was it?

➥ **He opened Montreal's very first bagel bakery.** The bagel, the ring-shaped baked good that has made Montreal famous (and tastes great with lox and cream cheese), was first introduced in Vienna in 1683, when a Jewish baker wanted to thank the King of Poland for rebuffing an invasion by the Turks. As his tribute to the king, he created a special, hard roll in the shape of a riding stirrup, which was called a "bugel" in German (horseback riding was a favourite pastime of the king).

When Seligman opened the Montreal Bagel Bakery in 1900, he sold the bagels on his horse-drawn cart and customers bought them on a string (which was the tradition in Russia).

In 1919, Isadore and Fanny Shlafman, Russian Jewish immigrants from Kiev, opened their own bagel shop (also called the Montreal Bagel Bakery), which was located in a wooden shack in a narrow lane near Schwartz's delicatessen on St. Lawrence Boulevard. Using a recipe from his native Kiev (rings of yeast dough soaked in sweet water and baked in a brick oven powered by firewood), Shlafman transported the freshly baked bagels in a wheelbarrow and sold them at a stand on St. Lawrence Boulevard for 5 cents each.

St-Viateur Bagel Shop founder Mayer Lewkowitz, with the bagels that made his shop famous (circa 1988).

How popular are Montreal bagels? Joe King in *From the Ghetto to the Main: The Story of the Jews of Montreal* recounts this story: "The St. Viateur bakery received a call one evening, saying 'Prince Charles would like to order 20 dozen bagels.' The owner responded: 'It's Saturday night, we're busy, so stop fooling around.' An hour later, a fleet of limousines pulled up and a British naval officer marched into the store. 'I'm here,' he announced grandly, 'for Prince Charles' bagels.' The clerk's reaction was brusque: 'You'll have to wait like everybody else.' It was, after all, a very busy night. The officer had to wait an hour while the limousines remained parked outside. Prince Charles, heir to the throne, was in Montreal Port aboard a naval warship, waiting patiently for Montreal bagels."

With an influx of immigrants arriving in Montreal from Europe following World War II (mainly Holocaust survivors), an increased demand for the East European bagel was created. This prompted Shlafman to open Fairmount Bagel out of the living room of his home on Fairmount Street in 1950. Seven years later, Shlafman's son Jack joined up with Mayer Lewkowitz, a Holocaust survivor who worked as a baker for Seligman, to open the Fairmount Bagel Bakery on St-Viateur Street. The original Fairmount Bagel shop closed in 1959. The following year, Jack Shlafman and baker Isaac Schneider left the St-Viateur shop to open another bagel bakery, which became Van Horne Bagel in 1961.

In 1979, as bagels were quickly becoming a popular staple for breakfast and brunch, and after seeing the steady stream of customers at the renamed St-Viateur Bagel Shop, Jack Shlafman and his family reopened Fairmount Bagel at its original Fairmount Street location. They found the original wood-burning oven preserved inside a false wall along with the original baking utensils.

What makes the Montreal bagel distinctive compared to its Toronto and New York counterparts? It is sweeter and is baked in a wood-fired oven, compared to the gas-fired bakery ovens that are used in bakeries in Toronto and New York. They also look much thicker and heavier. Montreal writer Barry Lazar claims that what makes the Montreal bagel unique is its "temperament". "It must be coddled in sweet, hot water and tempered in fire. It retains a crunch at the first bite and a malty flavor within. It freezes well and reheats beautifully in a toaster oven."

## What is the name of the unsuccessful restaurant that mayor Drapeau opened at the Windsor Hotel in 1969?

→Le Vaisseau D'Or. Until then, Jean Drapeau had made his name in Montreal as a lawyer, a racket buster and a mayor . . . but as a restaurateur? Inspired by his favourite restaurant in Paris called Sheherezade (named after the storytelling character from the Arabian Nights), Drapeau decided to open a high-class restaurant at the Windsor Hotel called Le Vaisseau D'Or, or the Golden Vessel.

Named after a poem by Quebecois poet Émile Nelligan, Le Vaisseau D'Or was made to resemble the living room of a large Montreal mansion in the late 1890s. It featured seven-course meals at $10 a person, drinks and appetizers at $2 each, $6.50 bottles of wine (of which there was a choice of six), and a $9 bottle of champagne. To top it all off, a 21-piece symphony orchestra featuring a selection of baroque, classical and romantic music played twice a night at 7:30 p.m. and 10 p.m. And owing to the gilded atmosphere it was trying to promote, Le Vaisseau D'Or had a strict rule that patrons had to speak in low tones of voice and put their wine and food orders in writing to the waiters.

And while he spent his days conducting civic affairs at City Hall, Drapeau spent his evenings shuttling to the Windsor Hotel to oversee the arrangements for the restaurant's grand opening.

Criticized that his position as mayor gave him an unfair advantage over competing restaurants and that his venture might be causing him to neglect his duties at City Hall, Drapeau finally opened Le Vaisseau D'Or on September 8, 1969. *The Montreal Star* was rather cynical about the mayor's new profession as a restaurateur: "If you haven't learned yet to swallow your soup in silence, chances are you may well be persona non grata at mayor Drapeau's new restaurant. And if Bach and Vivaldi mean little to you then it's a fair gamble as to whether wining and dining will be worth the possible $30 or $40 per couple an evening at Le Vaisseau D'Or."

The grand opening, which attracted Quebec cabinet ministers, Montreal's diplomatic corps, top city officials and the cream of Montreal's elite, was a fiasco. Three hours into the event, about one-third of the 280 invitees left the restaurant frustrated and hungry, having not yet been served. Another third of the guests were served only two out of the seven promised courses. According to *The Toronto Star,* Drapeau was "looking pale and nervous, stood by as setback after setback kept marring what should have been the grand opening of one of his great projects."

After the disastrous opening night, things settled down, but not for the better. At best, the restaurant was only half-full on most nights. Many patrons only attended once for the chance to meet Drapeau, who greeted guests from table to table. But the bad service and the rule of silence discouraged them from paying a return visit. Le Vaisseau D'Or also became a target for angry mobs, citizen groups, tenement associations, and striking taxi drivers and firemen, who viewed Le Vaisseau D'Or as a symbol of Drapeau's excesses.

e Vaisseau D'or was notorious for its very slow service. One irate customer wrote: "Our group arrived at 7:05, a half-hour late, we feared, for the dinner which was supposed to start at 6:30, but not too late for the first cocktail, which didn't arrive until 7:50. By 8:30, a little bread and music. Hope sprang up at 8:45 when a waiter apologized for the delay in bringing our dinner. It was 9 when he showed up with hors d'oeuvres. At 9:05 came our wine. Hope began to fade by 9:35. At 10 we left — and went home to soup and scrambled eggs."

By 1970, Drapeau was behind in the rent that he owed the Windsor Hotel's multi-millionaire owner Howard Webster. Webster threatened to close down the restaurant if business did not improve but was persuaded to be patient until after November. It was an election year and any attempt to foreclose during the campaign would be seen as embarrassing to Drapeau politically and would hurt his chances for re-election.

On January 4, 1971, Drapeau announced that Le Vaisseau D'Or would be closing, but only temporarily in order "to improve the décor, service and format". Denying that the closing was due to the financial problems he was having with Webster, Drapeau said he was going to examine client suggestions and hoped to make the restaurant more pleasant, install certain kitchen equipment and bring it "closer to the people". He targeted a reopening date of March that year. Le Vaisseau D'Or never reopened.

## What popular Montreal restaurant, which closed suddenly in 1959 due to an exercise in city planning, was modelled after an old-fashioned English inn?

➡**Drury's.** Regarded as one of the oldest and best-known restaurants in Montreal, Drury's was opened in 1868 by John Drury. Located on Windsor Street between Osborne and St-Antoine streets, the original Drury's catered to the growing tourist trade.

In 1887, with the completion of the Windsor Hotel and Windsor Station (which would help bring in more tourists), Drury's moved to a new location on Osborne Street facing the southern end of Dominion Square . . . this time, as a fancy restaurant. The new location was made to resemble an old-fashioned 16th century English inn and chophouse. Edgar Andrew Collard, former Gazette columnist and historian, described Drury's as having tall windows of opaque-coloured glass, old-fashioned lamps, tall wooden doors, and an interior that "had kept much of the atmosphere of an old house . . . the dark panelling of the walls, the large chairs with their high backs and leather upholstery, tacked with brass, [which] contributed to the mood of the chophouse solidity."

A favourite with patrons who enjoyed good food, fine wine and a relaxed atmosphere, Drury's quickly became a popular restaurant. It also attracted celebrities such as comedian Jack Benny, former First Lady Eleanor Roosevelt, British Prime Minister Sir Anthony Eden, actors Raymond Massey and Mary Pickford, conductor Leopold Stokowski, and New York City mayor Fiorello LaGuardia.

During World War II, Drury's had a well-stocked wine cellar at a time when frugality was a way of life. It was able to sell brandy — which was scarce at the time — at $3 per glass or $40 per bottle.

In 1938, John Drury's son Jimmy sold the restaurant to Leo Dandurand, a Montreal sports promoter who was best known as the former coach and owner of the Montreal Canadiens. He ran Drury's for over 20 years and maintained its reputation as one of the most popular restaurants in the city. It became the site of many Canadiens' Stanley Cup victory parties and, according to 1950s Gazette columnist "Fitz", was the place where "many a Montreal marriage got started . . . and many a Montreal business deal."

By the late 1950s, Drury's fell victim to City Hall's ambitious development plans. The restaurant was situated in one of the most expensive pieces of land in Montreal and became a target of mayor Sarto Fournier's street improvement plan, in which Osborne and Lagauchetière streets would be linked. On October 22, 1959, the city expropriated the land and ordered that Drury's be closed up by November 30.

Customers were shocked at City Hall's rush judgment regarding Drury's fate. A petition was sent to Quebec Premier Paul Sauvé, urging him to stop the expropriation, but nothing was done. Dandurand was also very angered over the sudden closing. "It made you think you were living in a Communist country, the way it was done," he told *The Gazette*.

During its last week of business, many loyal patrons crowded the restaurant. Many of them left with a piece of Drury's to take home as mementoes such as sugar bowls, salt and pepper shakers and pieces of silverware. Drury's served its last meal at midnight on November 28, 1959. One week later, many of its fixtures — such as chairs, tables, stained glass windows and brass rails — were auctioned off to a group of 25 restaurant and bar owners (the unsold pieces were sent to Café Martin, which was also owned by Dandurand). The building was later torn down.

The southern end of Dominion Square where Drury's stood became Place du Canada in the mid 1960s, and Osborne Street was phased out of existence shortly afterward.

# LITTLE TOWN OF VILLE-MARIE

## montreal — the early years

**What was the name of the famous dog that helped defend Ville-Marie against the Iroquois?**

➥**Pilotte.** In its early days, the Ville-Marie settlement was under constant attack by Iroquois warriors. The Iroquois saw the French settlers as rivals. They regarded their practice of trading goods between the Huron and Algonquin tribes in Trois-Rivières as a threat to their own role as go-betweens for aboriginal tribes in the west. The Iroquois believed that by harassing the French, they could drive them back to France and retain control of the fur trade.

The first attack occurred on June 9, 1643, when the Iroquois attacked the Ville-Marie colony and killed and scalped three of its settlers. They also captured three prisoners, two of whom were later burned at the stake. The third escaped and returned to the colony.

Paul de Chomedey de Maisonneuve, the colony's founder, initiated several measures of protection for Ville-Marie. He established a contingent of musket-armed sentinels to patrol the fort, recruited Huron and Algonquin scouts, got 40 soldiers from France as reinforcements, and renovated the fort's walls. In the fall of 1643, de Maisonneuve began using dogs owned by Madame de la Peltrie, the founder of the Ursulines convent, to patrol the outskirts of the settlement, sniffing out potential aggressors. Pilotte was the leader of the band of dogs. When Pilotte and the other dogs detected Iroquois fighters, they would bark and howl as loudly as possible to warn the settlers.

Pilotte's contribution to Ville-Marie's survival is immortalized on the statue of de Maisonneuve standing at Place d'Armes. Below de Maisonneuve's figure, in the southeast corner of the monument, is militia commander Lambert Closse, and underneath his left arm, is his valiant canine scout Pilotte.

Attacks ended in August of 1701 when a peace treaty was signed between the French and the Iroquois.

Born in Chambly, Marie-Louise-Cécile-Emma Lajeunesse, an opera singer, was one of the first Montreal-based personalities to become an international superstar. She gained worldwide fame as well as the admiration of crowned heads of Europe such as Kaiser Wilhelm I, Tsar Alexander II, and Queen Victoria. What was Lajeunesse's stage name?

➥**Madame Emma Albani.** Marie-Louise-Cécile-Emma Lajeunesse was born on November 1, 1852. Her father, Joseph Lajeunesse, was a church organist and a versatile yet unsuccessful musician. Emma began to read music at the age of five. Under her father's tutelage, she became proficient at the piano, organ and harp, and by the time she was eight, Emma could sight-read major musical works by contemporary and classical composers.

But it was her voice that made Lajeunesse the centre of attention. As a student at Montreal's Convent of the Sacred Heart, she won every music contest held by the school. At the age of 15, Lajeunesse left the convent to join St. Joseph's Roman Catholic Church in Albany, New York, where she worked as the church's organist, choir conductor, and first soprano. Her singing quickly developed a huge following in Albany. Through the auspices of St. Joseph's Bishop Conroy, a series of benefit concerts were organized to allow her to pursue her musical studies in Europe.

Lajeunesse studied music in Paris and Milan. It was here that she chose her stage name of Emma Albani. Before her professional operatic debut in 1870, one of her music teachers suggested that she use the name Madame Albani "out of compliment to a family he had known for many years but which had died out". She agreed, thinking it would also be a form of tribute to the city and people of Albany, where she had made her first public appearance as a singer.

Starting in 1872, Albani began performing in Europe to wide acclaim. She received 25 curtain calls during a performance in Russia and, prior to an appearance in Dublin, more than 6,000 fans gathered outside her hotel.

*Internationally renowned opera singer (and friend of Queen Victoria) Emma Albani.*

Perhaps her greatest fan was none other than Queen Victoria of England. She not only became one of Albani's closest friends but also her most enthusiastic supporter.

Although her career took her across Europe, Albani never forgot her Montreal roots. In March of 1883, she returned to perform in Montreal and received an overwhelming welcome. Her performance at the Queen's Hall Theatre was to a sold-out crowd with some audience members spilling out onto the stage.

Emma Albani made her final Montreal concert appearance on April 9, 1906, when she appeared at the Mount Royal Arena as part of her farewell Canadian tour. She continued to perform until 1912 and then held her farewell concert at the Royal Albert Hall in London. When she ended the performance with her rendition of Tosti's "Good-Bye", the 10,000 people in attendance were reduced to tears.

Albani spent her retirement years in London, where she had been living since 1872. However, she never denied her Canadian roots. "I have married an Englishman, and have made my home in England, but I still remain at heart a French Canadian," she said.

Emma Albani died in London on April 3, 1930, at the age of 77. Her birthplace in Chambly was deemed a historic site by the federal Historic Sites and Monuments Commission and in 1980, on the 50th anniversary of her death, Canada Post issued a commemorative stamp in her honour.

# What future British monarch officially dedicated the Victoria Bridge during a royal visit to Canada and the United States in 1860?

↪ **The Prince of Wales,** who became King Edward VII in 1901.

The Victoria Bridge, the first bridge to cross the St. Lawrence River, was conceived in 1847 and construction began 10 years later.

By the time the 9,184 foot-long bridge was opened on December 12, 1859, it was hoped that Queen Victoria herself would travel to Montreal to officially open it. Instead, the task fell upon her eldest son Edward Albert, the Prince of Wales, who would make the official dedication as one of the stops of his 1860 tour of North America.

**W**hile the Victoria Bridge was being built in the late 1850s, Queen Victoria asked Sir George-Étienne Cartier how many feet it was in length from shore to shore. Cartier replied: "When we Canadians build a bridge and dedicate it to your majesty, we measure it, not in feet, but in miles!"

The City of Montreal greeted the Prince of Wales' upcoming visit with much excitement. The provincial government gave a grant of $20,000 to defray the costs of the visit, and the city kicked in $10,000, along with an additional $2,000 to spruce up Viger Square. But that was not the only part of Montreal that was spruced up for the prince's visit. Streets were paved, houses painted, ferries given a new coat of whitewash, trees planted, and fountains were placed in many of the city's squares. Montreal was decorated with flags, banners, flowers, evergreens, and arches.

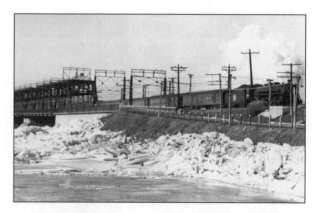

*A passenger train crosses the Victoria Bridge in 1950, exactly 90 years after the future King Edward VII officially dedicated the bridge.*

*The Prince of Wales (Edward VII) in 1860, at the time of his royal visit to Montreal.*

For the royal visit, Montreal mayor Charles Rodier ordered himself a set of mayoral robes that resembled those of the Lord Mayor of London. The scarlet ermine-trimmed robe also included a cocked hat, chain of office, and dress sword.

The Prince of Wales arrived on August 25, 1860, aboard the steamer *Kingston*. That afternoon, he laid the bridge's last stone and drove in the final rivet (made of silver). He was then presented with a gold medal especially struck by the Grand Trunk Railway for the occasion. The performance of a specially written grand cantata by the 400-voice Montreal Oratorio Society followed.

The social highlight of the visit happened that evening. A grand ball was held at the newly opened Crystal Palace in downtown Montreal. Nearly 6,000 people attended the gala affair in the 3,000-foot diameter venue lit by 2,000 gas lamps, and which had fountains that spewed out rosewater, eau de cologne and lavender, flowing champagne, claret, and lemonade. The prince was seen dancing until the ball ended at 4:30 a.m.

Forty-one years later, the royal connection to the Victoria Bridge came full circle. On October 16, 1901, Edward VII's oldest son, the Duke of York (who later became King George V), inaugurated the newly renovated Victoria Bridge.

# What famous English author produced and starred in a theatrical revue show at the Theatre Royal during a visit to Montreal in 1842?

→**Charles Dickens.** The author of such classic novels as *Oliver Twist, Nicholas Nickelby* and *A Christmas Carol,* Dickens made his fortune by travelling around the world reading excerpts from his works at theatres and concert halls.

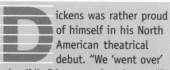 ickens was rather proud of himself in his North American theatrical debut. "We 'went over' splendidly," he wrote in a letter. "I really do believe that I was funny." One Montreal critic shared his enthusiasm, saying that the three-part revue was "a sort of mixture of the late Charles Matthews [a popular English comic actor during the early 1800s] and Mr. [John Baldwin] Buckstone's" (a renowned English comedian and dramatist of the 1830s and 1840s).

In 1842, Dickens embarked on a six-city reading tour of the United States where he played to full houses with live readings of *David Copperfield, The Pickwick Papers* and *Martin Chuzzlewit.* He decided to spend the tail end of his tour in Canada and visited Niagara Falls, Toronto, and Montreal.

He arrived in Montreal on May 12 and, for the next 18 days, settled in at the famous Rasco's Hotel on St-Paul Street. During his stay, the Governor General, members of the British Garrison, and many of Montreal's prominent citizens vied for the opportunity to entertain Dickens and his wife. However, Dickens spent most of his time in Montreal organizing the British Garrison's amateur theatrical revue, acting as its manager, producer, and lead actor. Dickens loved this flirtation with the world of theatre and relished the task of putting a show together.

The fruit of Dickens' labours culminated in a performance at the Theatre Royal at the corner of St-Paul and Bonsecours streets on May 25, 1842, in front of an audience of 600 people. The three-part revue consisted of *A Roland for an Oliver,* which featured Dickens and his tour shipmate Lord Mulgrave, *Past Two O'Clock in the Morning,* a French one-scene play that also starred Dickens, and a one-act farce called *Deaf as a Post,* in which Mrs. Dickens participated. Proceeds from the show benefited several Montreal charities, including the Montreal General Hospital.

Dickens left Montreal on May 29 after a brief visit to New York and Quebec City, satisfied that he had dazzled Montreal audiences with his acting abilities.

**What presidential assassin spent several weeks as a guest at Montreal's prestigious St. Lawrence Hall Hotel, as he put together the plot that would lead to the death of the 16th President of the United States?**

➥**John Wilkes Booth.** During the years leading up to the US Civil War and during the war itself, Montreal was sympathetic to the rebel southern Confederate States of America. Going against Queen Victoria's instruction at the outbreak of the war stating that her colonies were to observe absolute neutrality, Montreal became the unofficial headquarters for Confederate spies and sympathizers. Its close location to the US border and its state as a neutral territory made it an ideal haven for Southern infiltrators planning and carrying out acts of terrorism and sabotage against the North.

A favourite hangout for these rebel spies was St. Lawrence Hall, a fashionable hotel on St-James Street near Place d'Armes. One of the most notorious guests at St. Lawrence Hall was John Wilkes Booth, an actor born of a prominent acting family that dominated American theatre during the 19th century. A strong Southern sympathizer, Booth came to Montreal in April of 1865. During his stay, he kept a journal of what transacted during a series of meetings between himself and other Lincoln conspirators at the hotel, which culminated with the assassination of the president.

Opened in 1851, St. Lawrence Hall was run by Henry Hogan, a genial individual whose main wish was to make sure that all of his guests were well fed and comfortable. Quickly, his hotel became world famous. In addition, St. Lawrence Hall served as the headquarters for British officers stationed in Montreal, was the main site for the negotiations that established the Grand Trunk Railway, and was the location chosen to house the Prince of Wales' staff during his visit to Montreal in 1860.

While in Montreal, Booth did not attempt to conceal the fact that he was a professional actor from a distinguished acting family, and gave the impression that he was seeking acting jobs at the Theatre Royal. However, while in social situations, Booth had a tendency to drink a little too much and would not hesitate to share his plot against Lincoln to any companion caring to listen. One of those listeners was a guest from Ontario who learned of the plot over a game of billiards with Booth.

Booth told the unsuspecting pool partner: "Do you know I have got the sharpest play laid out over in America. I can bag the biggest game . . . It made damned little difference head or tail . . . Abe's contract was near up and whether re-elected or not, he would get his goose cooked."

Booth's poolroom confidant did not think much of this covert plot to kill Lincoln. In fact, he thought it was more of an indication of "a slight mental derangement or excitement".

On April 29, 1865, more than two weeks after Lincoln's assassination and Booth's death in an abandoned Virginia farmhouse, a man suspected to be Booth was arrested at the Garneau Hotel in Montreal. Police refused to believe that Booth had been killed by federal troops and believed he had escaped to Montreal. The suspect, who bore an uncanny resemblance to Booth, refused to acknowledge that he was Lincoln's assassin. Booth's double was taken to the main police station at Bonsecours Market and was searched, questioned and released by police superintendent Charles-Joseph Coursol, who was also a Confederate sympathizer. The police never revealed the name of Booth's double.

## The assassination of what Father of Confederation in 1868 led to one of the largest funerals ever held in Montreal?

→Thomas D'Arcy McGee. Born in Ireland in 1825, McGee crossed the Atlantic in 1848 and became a journalist in New York, where he wrote numerous articles against the city's Catholic hierarchy. He later moved to Boston, where he proceeded to alienate himself from the radical Irish Party.

In the spring of 1857, McGee was invited by Montreal's Irish community to speak on their behalf. Once in Montreal, he established a publication called *New Era,* which advocated political and cultural nationalism and Canadian independence. McGee quickly established himself as a reformist and found Montreal more accommodating to Irish Catholics.

By the 1860s, McGee became a moderate Tory and, in 1863, was appointed to John A. Macdonald's cabinet. An eloquent, fiery speaker, McGee was a firm believer in bringing together all components that made up British North America and strongly pushed for confederation. Montreal's Irish community stood by him.

A New York-based organization called the Fenian Brotherhood disagreed with McGee. Founded in 1854 by a group of exiled Irish nationalists, the Fenians believed that Ireland could be liberated from the British through an armed insurrection. They hoped that by conduct-

*Journalist, politician and Father of Confederation Thomas D'Arcy McGee. Over 100,000 people lined the streets of Montreal for his funeral in 1868.*

ing an armed invasion of Canada from their base in New York State, that they could draw the United States into a war with Britain. McGee condemned the Fenians and called them "a political leprosy" and urged his fellow Irishmen to avoid them "as you would the jaws of hell". Before the 1867 federal election, McGee wrote a series of articles, published in *The Gazette,* which exposed the rise of the Fenian movement in Montreal. He urged his readers to support his anti-Fenian stance and "extinguish the hopes of the clique of Fenian conspirators who still remain in Canada".

In 1867, McGee won his Montreal West riding seat by 262 votes and chose to leave his post in Macdonald's cabinet. He believed he could better serve the cause of Canadian unity as a Member of Parliament. He used the House of Commons as a forum to promote unity issues and continued herein to oppose the Fenians.

In early April of 1868, McGee told Gazette editor Brown Chamberlain, rather prophetically, that "if ever I were murdered it would be by some wretch who would shoot me from behind".

The Montreal Gazette marvelled at the spectacle that was D'Arcy McGee's funeral: ". . . never since Jacques Cartier first planted the foot of a European on the site on which now stands the great city of Montreal, was there ever before a demonstration, either funeral or other, within its borders such as that which took place yesterday . . . nothing could better demonstrate how profoundly the great heart of society is moved by the tragic event that has occurred, or how deep had sunk into men's hearts affliction and love for him whom we mourn".

A few days later, on April 7, Thomas D'Arcy McGee was shot in the back of the head by Fenian James Patrick Whelan. His lifeless body was found outside his rooming house on Sparks Street in Ottawa with a half-smoked cigar clenched between his teeth. He was only 42 years old.

Montreal mayor William Workman ordained that a public funeral be held in his honour. More than 100,000 citizens crowded the Montreal streets to view the funeral procession.

The procession was a grandiose affair. McGee's coffin was placed on a carriage pulled by six grey horses draped in black. On the carriage were symbols of McGee's Irish background including his family's coat of arms, a silver harp, and a shamrock. The coffin was placed on a platform surrounded by a tent-shaped canopy and bore a large white cross supported by eight carved pillars. On either side of the platform were silver plates, one with McGee's name and date of death, the other with the last poem that he wrote.

McGee's body lay in state for three days in the dining room of his home on St-Catherine Street, after which he was interred in the family vault at the Cote des Neiges Cemetery, facing west toward Ottawa.

Whelan was tried, convicted of McGee's murder, and hanged in February of 1869.

**François Dollier de Casson, Superior of the Sulpician Order during Montreal's colonial days in the late 17th century, served as a militia officer and helped build the Sulpician Seminary that still stands on Notre-Dame Street. What else did Dollier de Casson accomplish in 1672?**

➥**He wrote and published the first history of the city.** Written in the winter of 1672–1673, *The History of Montreal* covered the first 30 years of the Ville-Marie settlement and its evolution into the City of Montreal. Dollier de Casson was an ideal chronicler of the city's early history as he had witnessed many events, notably the skirmishes with the Iroquois. He also spoke to many of the surviving settlers who helped Paul de Chomedey de Maisonneuve establish Ville-Marie in 1642.

The narrative is more lively than scholarly. Dollier de Casson recounted the story of numerous everyday people such as Madame Primot, who fended off potential Iroquois attackers with her hands and feet, rather than a pistol or musket. The book was also the first to give future generations a record of Montreal's first permanent settlers, such as de Maisonneuve, Lambert Closse, and Jeanne Mance.

Dollier de Casson had many talents. In addition to his writing skills and his successful career in the militia, he was also a respected city planner. In March of 1672, with the help of surveyor Benigne Basset, he laid out Montreal's first streets. He determined the streets' width and established the location of adjoining property lines, with Notre-Dame Street as its main artery. Many of the streets still exist today and form part of Old Montreal. These include St-Paul Street (in honour of de Maisonneuve) and St-François Xavier Street (in honour of himself).

François Dollier de Casson died in 1701 in the Sulpician Seminary that he helped build between 1672 and 1685. This building still stands today as Montreal's oldest building and now houses a private retirement home for members of the clergy.

n his book *The History of Montreal,* Dollier de Casson writes about an unusual skirmish that took place around the fall of 1651 between three Iroquois warriors and a Ville-Marie settler named Madame Primot, whom Dollier de Casson described as "a woman of virtue": "As soon as she was attacked she shouted loudly; at this three hidden bodies of Iroquois appeared and three of these savages threw themselves upon her to kill her with their hatchets. At this, the woman defended herself like a lioness, but as she had no weapons but hands and feet, at the third or fourth blow they felled her as if dead. Immediately one of the Iroquois flung himself upon her to scalp her and escape with this shameful trophy. But as our amazon felt herself so seized, she at once recovered her senses, raised herself and, more fierce than ever, caught hold of this monster so forcibly by a place which modestly forbids us to mention that he could not free himself." Madame Primot survived the attack.

In 1775–1776, a delegation led by US statesman Benjamin Franklin arrived in Montreal and attempted to convince French Canadians to side with them in the American Revolution. One of these men was a French-born printer named Fleury Mesplet. What Montreal newspaper did Mesplet go on to found?

➥ *The Montreal Gazette.*

In February of 1776, the Continental Congress of the United States established a three-man commission led by newspaper publisher/ statesman Benjamin Franklin. This commission was given as a task to go to Montreal and investigate the military situation therein, improve relations with its inhabitants and, most importantly, convince Montrealers to support the cause against the British during the Revolutionary War.

This goal was a difficult one. Montreal had been under American control since 1775 and, following the death of General Richard Montgomery, a well-respected American leader by Montrealers, was being controlled by General David Wooster, a non-diplomatic man who openly despised French Canadians.

Local merchants refused to do business with the occupying army. In January of 1776, General Wooster responded by posting an order stating that anyone who spoke out against the Continental Congress would be banished from the province.

The commission arrived on April 27, 1776. Franklin, who was given a wide range of absolute powers by the Congress, established his headquarters at the Château de Ramezay. Fleury Mesplet, a printer by trade, produced pamphlets trying to recruit French-speaking residents to their cause. However, the Montreal population knew Mesplet as a fervent supporter of the Americans since 1774 and did not offer support.

Franklin believed the mission futile due to the damage and resentment created by the ineffectual command of General Wooster. As well, because the majority of Montreal's English-speaking residents continued to be loyal to the British, Franklin chose to leave. One month later, in June of 1776, the British recaptured Montreal.

Mesplet was left behind in Montreal, with no money and only a printing press to his name. He was arrested by the British for serving under the Americans during the occupation and served 26 days in jail. Upon his release, the British used Mesplet and his press to publish Montreal's first books. The result was a 40-page booklet written by the

Sulpicians called *Réglement de la Confrérie de l'Adoration Perpétuelle du Saint-Sacrement et de la Bonne Mort,* as well as the text of a tragic play called *Jonatas et David.*

But Mesplet was ambitious and wanted to launch a periodical of his own. With funds borrowed from a friend, and with the collaboration of journalist and notary Valentin Jautard, Mesplet printed the first edition of the *Gazette du Commerce et Littéraire (The Commercial and Literary Gazette)* on June 3, 1778. Jautard was named the paper's first editor-in-chief.

On June 2, 1779, as a result of the numerous complaints lodged by readers against Jautard's writings, which were critical of the church, the city's judges, and the court system, Sir Frederick Haldimand, Montreal's British governor, arrested Mesplet and Jautard and suspended publication of *The Gazette*. Mesplet was released from jail in 1782 and returned to Montreal. Three years later, he revived the paper under the name *The Montreal Gazette/La Gazette de Montréal* and published it as a bilingual paper. It was well received by readers from Montreal to Quebec City.

n the first issue, Mesplet wrote a statement of principles that stated that *The Gazette* would be a newspaper that would serve the public's interests at large, whether it be selling merchandise, furniture or property, finding lost personal property or "capturing runaway Negroes". The first issue of *The Gazette* was available in French only, consisted of four pages, and was the size of a book. It was not sold by single copy, but by subscription for two and a half Spanish dollars per year.

Fleury Mesplet died on January 22, 1794, at the age of 60. *The Gazette* once again ceased publication on February 13, after his widow tried to run the operation. In July of 1795, it was taken over by an English publisher named Edward Edwards. It remained a bilingual paper until 1822, when publisher Thomas Andrew Turner announced that *The Gazette* would be published in English only. A weekly newspaper since its inception in 1778, *The Gazette* became a year-round daily publication in 1853.

**On February 15, 1839, a group of 12 Patriotes were hung at what east end prison for their participation in the Lower Canada Rebellion of 1837–1838?**

→ **Pied-du-Courant Prison.**

In 1837, Lower Canada's French-speaking population felt unfairly treated. Out of 500,000 French Canadian citizens, only a minority served in Lower Canada's legislature and judiciary system. Between 1800 and 1830, only 11 of 30 Lower Canada judges were francophone, and only 54 of 126 civil servants were French speaking. Wages were also uneven: 28,000 livres per year compared to 58,000 livres paid to English-speaking civil servants.

Meetings were held to denounce the government, to encourage the support of Patriote leader Louis-Joseph Papineau, and to boycott goods imported from Britain. Two groups were created as a result of the growing unrest: the pro-French Fils de la Liberté (Sons of Liberty, or Patriotes) and the pro-British Doric Club. While Papineau advocated caution and a constitutional solution, Wolfred Nelson, another Fils leader and future mayor of Montreal, told his followers: "The time has come for us to melt our spoons into bullets."

Although the 1837–1838 Rebellion in Lower Canada was effectively quelled by the British, its legacy remained. In 1858, the liberal Institut Canadien erected a monument at Cote des Neiges Cemetery with the names of all the Patriotes who were exiled, executed, and died in the skirmishes against British troops. On June 24, 1926, a monument to the memory of the Patriotes was unveiled on the corner of Delorimier and Notre-Dame streets by the Lieutenant Governor of Quebec and Madame Marion Cardinal, the daughter of Joseph-Narcisse Cardinal, the first Patriote executed at Pied-du-Courant in December of 1838.

On November 16, 1837, the Patriotes took up arms against the British. This led to the Lower Canada Rebellion, in which bloody battles at St-Denis, St-Charles and St-Eustache killed 120 Patriotes.

On December 5, 1837, Governor General Lord Gosford declared martial law in Montreal and gave its military commander Sir John Colborne the authority to arrest, put to death or punish anyone who had any connection with the Rebellion. A total of 698 arrests were made and special efforts had to be made to rush the completion of the new Pied-du-Courant Prison to accommodate them.

A second rebellion erupted in 1838 in La Prairie, south of Montreal, but the pitchfork-wielding farmers were no match for Colborne's 5,000 troops and were crushed immediately.

In April 1838, 112 Patriotes were brought before a military tribunal and justice was swift. Sixty-six of them were exiled to Bermuda and Australia, 12 were acquitted, 30 were released on bail, and 12 were sentenced to hang at Pied-du-Courant. Papineau and Nelson fled to the United States. Nelson was captured and returned to Montreal, and a death sentence was levied upon Papineau in absentia, but was later annulled.

The first two of the 12 condemned Patriotes were hung at Pied-du-Courant on December 12, 1838, followed by five more on January 18, 1839. The final five were hung on February 15, 1839. The most prominent of the Patriotes hung was notary François-Marie-Thomas Chevalier De Lorimier, whose last words were: "Can my country ever forget that we die for her upon the scaffold? We have lived as Patriotes — as Patriotes let us die. Down with the tyrants! Their reign is over!"

Pied-du-Courant Prison still stands in Montreal's east end at the foot of the Jacques Cartier Bridge. It now serves as the headquarters of the Quebec Liquor Commission. Here, yearly on February 15, a ceremony is held in memory of the 12 Patriotes who met their deaths within its walls.

**In 1929, what Montreal-born writer/women's rights activist won an appeal brought before the Privy Council that gave women the right to sit in the Canadian Senate?**

→**Henrietta Louise Muir Edwards.** Born in Montreal on December 18, 1849, Edwards, along with her sister, founded the Working Girls' Association in 1875, which was a combination boarding house, reading room and vocational training center for Montreal women, and which was a precursor for the Young Women's Christian Association (YWCA). She also edited *Working Woman of Canada,* a journal oriented toward women's issues, recognized as the earliest publication of its kind in Canada.

In addition to marrying Dr. Oliver Cromwell Edwards, moving to Alberta and raising three children, Henrietta Louise Muir Edwards became known as an authority on laws for women and children, and fought for the equal rights of parents and for mother's allowances. In 1893, she and Lady Aberdeen, the wife of then Governor General of

Canada Lord Aberdeen, founded the National Council of Women of Canada, the oldest advocacy organization in Canada, and served as its vice president, and later as convenor for its standing committee on laws affecting women and children, a position she held for more than 35 years. In the 1920s, she also wrote two books dealing with the legal status of women in both Alberta and Canada.

In 1920, Edwards became part of a group called the Alberta Five, along with Judge Emily Murphy, Irene Parlby, a member of the Alberta cabinet, Louise McKinney, a former member of the Alberta legislature, and Nellie McClung, a feminist, author and legislator. They introduced an appeal to the Supreme Court of Canada that challenged the following section of the British North America (BNA) Act, which stated that the Governor General shall "summon qualified persons to the Senate; and subject to the provisions of this act every person so summoned shall become, and be, a member of the Senate and a Senator." However, when the BNA Act was passed in 1867, the term "qualified persons" did not apply to women, and therefore, they were not allowed to sit in the Canadian Senate. In August of 1928, the Supreme Court of Canada rejected the group's appeal and upheld the Act's interpretation of the word "persons".

n 1929, when the Privy Council ruled in favour of the Alberta Five, which deemed women as "persons" and allowed them to be Senators, the Canadian Senate had five vacancies: two each from Ontario and Quebec, and one from Manitoba. Prime Minister William Lyon Mackenzie King hoped to appoint one or two women to fill those vacancies. As of 2001, 31 women serve as Senators, and 60 women as Members of Parliament.

Undaunted, the Alberta Five brought their case to the Privy Council in London, which at the time was the highest court in the land dealing with Canadian legal matters. On October 18, 1929, the Privy Council ruled in favour of the Alberta Five, stating that the word "persons" was vague and ambiguous in the BNA Act and "that the word persons includes members of both the male and female sex". This judgment permitted women to finally serve in the Canadian Senate and was met with a great deal of praise and enthusiasm by women all across Canada. Edwards was just as enthusiastic about the Privy Council's decision and looked ahead on the next issue that was of concern to Canadian women: "The next step to be accomplished is the personal naturalization of the married women. It is absurd that a woman is often called upon at the altar to choose between her country and her lover."

Henrietta Muir Edwards died in Macleod, Alberta, on November 10, 1931 at the age of 81. A plaque in her honour was placed in the Alberta Legislature Building in Edmonton. As well, her name and the name of the other members of the Alberta Five appear on a plaque at the entrance of the Senate chamber in Ottawa where, in 1929, they opened the door to future generations of women.

# TALES FROM THE
# GOLDEN SQUARE MILE

## montreal's merchant princes and business barons

From the 1930s to the 1980s, Steinberg's was one of the most important grocery store chains in Quebec. In 1957, Sam Steinberg introduced a new Steinberg customer promotion. What colourful name was this extremely popular promotion known as?

↪**Pinkys,** for the Pinky Stamps Program.

Ida Steinberg opened the first Steinberg's grocery store on St. Lawrence Boulevard in 1917. Her son Sam took over the family business and guided it to rapid expansion. By 1933, 10 stores were in business across Montreal.

In 1952, Sam Steinberg announced a five-year expansion plan in which a new store would open every 60 days, for a grand total of 30 stores. He also branched out into Montreal's growing suburbs. In the era of the baby boom, with low inflation rates and an economy where food sales where up 78 percent in Canada, the time was ripe. The first suburban Steinberg's was opened at the Dorval Gardens Shopping Centre in 1954. At the end of the five-year term, happy with the results of his venture, Steinberg announced the opening of an additional 60 stores in the following 36 months.

The widespread expansion also included several promotional schemes introduced by Sam Steinberg. These included opening cooking schools, launching a morning radio show called the *Steinberg Good Neighbour Club,* and offering gifts to brides and New Year's babies.

However, the most popular promotional scheme was the Pinky Stamps Program. Introduced in 1957, the program consisted of cashiers giving out pink cash register slips to customers who in turn would exchange them for an assortment of gifts with every $40 worth of pink slips. The program was successful through the 1960s.

Pinky stamps became a part of everyday life and have been immortalized in Michel Tremblay's classic play *Les Belles Soeurs,* in which a group of Quebecois housewives gather together to share their personal problems while pasting Pinky stamps into their stamp books.

The Pinky Stamps Program ended in the early 1970s. Sam Steinberg died in May of 1978 and, because of a running feud between his three daughters over the family business, the chain was sold in 1989 for $1.8 billion to Socanav Inc. Run by Quebec entrepreneur Michel Gaucher, Socanav was a company that had no experience in the grocery retail business. The Steinberg's chain folded shortly afterward.

**The Bronfman family is best known for its Seagram's whiskey distillery empire. In 1940, Samuel Bronfman decided to boost the morale of Canadians during the early years of World War II by privately publishing a history of Canada. Which legendary Canadian writer did Bronfman employ to write this book?**

➥**Stephen Leacock.** When World War II erupted in 1939, the Canadian government asked its country's distillers to mobilize and produce alcohol for military purposes. Samuel Bronfman and his Seagram's distillery were the first to jump on the patriotic bandwagon, producing smokeless powder and high-proof alcohol for synthetic rubber for the Canadian war effort.

Seagram's even produced a series of advertisements and posters to boost morale, and sold war bonds and stamps. But this was not enough for Bronfman. He was worried about morale on the home front and felt that school children knew very little about their country. He wanted to put together a book on the history of Canada that would be upbeat and patriotic in tone. To write it, Bronfman approached legendary writer, humorist, and former McGill University professor Stephen Leacock. Although he knew of Leacock's fervent opposition to prohibition and the hypocrisy of the temperance movement during World War I, Bronfman also overlooked the fact that Leacock was a racist who hated the rich and was anti-immigrant.

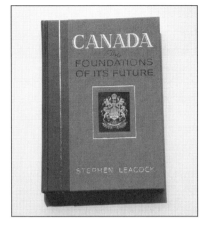

Stephen Leacock's 1940 book Canada: The Foundations of Its Future, *which was privately published by Samuel Bronfman as a morale booster. Even Joseph Stalin received an inscribed free copy.*

Leacock agreed to meet with Bronfman to discuss the book at his home in Orillia, Ontario, but under one condition: "Please tell him to bring a fishing rod". At the time, Leacock was desperately short on cash and agreed to write the book for $5,000 and promised to have the manuscript completed in four months.

When the manuscript was submitted to Seagram's, Bronfman was shocked to see that it was biased and that Leacock took swipes at immigrants, French Canadians, the Catholic Church, wealthy merchants, Americans, and the Irish. In addition, he ignored the contributions made by Eastern European immigrants to western Canada and urged that Canada not admit any more European immigrants after the war.

As a result, a series of intense negotiations over the text were held between Leacock and the Seagram's committee, led by poet Abraham Moses Klein. Leacock reluctantly agreed to many of the committee's points.

Copies of *Canada: The Foundations of Its Future* were given to numerous prominent personalities such as King George VI, the Duke of Windsor, Emperor Haile Selassie of Ethiopia, Jack Benny, and even Joseph Stalin. Poet and Seagram's committee head Abraham Moses Klein had the painstaking task of writing the dedications by hand in each copy, all of which were also signed by Bronfman. Klein's dedication to Stalin read:
"To Marshal Joseph Stalin,
Mighty leader, of mighty people, in war
So vigorous as in peace far-seeing,
Whose hammer pounds fascism, and
Whose scythe reaps freedom, this
History of his ally and neighbour is
Respectfully inscribed."

Bronfman supervised every aspect of the book's production, from the selection of the paper on which it was printed to the choice of printer and design. He also commissioned several Canadian artists to paint the 31 illustrations that would grace the book.

The book, entitled *Canada: The Foundations of Its Future,* was released on Mother's Day of 1942 in a handsome slipcased edition. Approximately 160,000 copies were printed privately by Seagram's and were distributed free of charge to schools, libraries, provincial and federal government officials, business executives, newspaper agencies, magazine publishing firms, bank managers, and service clubs across North America and Great Britain.

Nearly 40 years after its publication, the impact of *Canada: The Foundations of Its Future* was still felt. In June of 1972, one of the Bronfman companies, Cemp, applied to the Canadian Radio-Television and Telecommunications Commission (CRTC) for a television broadcast licence in Montreal. At the hearing on June 19, Bronfman lawyer Philip Vineberg quoted a passage from the book's foreword before he urged the commission to approve their application. The tactic was successful and the Bronfmans were granted the licence.

**In 1869, Hugh Graham founded a Montreal-based daily newspaper that would be regarded as Canada's greatest newspaper. But as of 1885, he used the newspaper as a platform for his crusade toward improving public health in Montreal. What was the name of this newspaper, and under what regal title was Graham better known as later in life?**

➥*The Montreal (Daily) Star,* **founded by Lord Atholstan.** Born in Huntingdon, Quebec in 1848, Graham left school at the age of 14 to work as an office boy for his uncle Edmund Henry Parsons, a popular journalist and publisher of two Montreal-based newspapers, *The Commercial Advertiser* and *The Evening Telegraph.*

Graham quickly worked his way up within the newspaper's management. In 1868, he teamed up with journalist George T. Lanigan to establish a new newspaper. On January 16, 1869, the first edition of *The Montreal Star* (then called *The Evening Star*) was published as a four-page paper costing a penny per copy. But Graham and Lanigan had conflicting viewpoints. Graham was a loyal imperialist, while Lanigan favoured annexation of Canada to the United States and wanted to use the paper to promote his opinions. Graham was adamantly opposed to this point of view and shortly afterwards, Lanigan left the paper, leaving Graham to run it alone.

With no financial help in sight, Graham and The Star faced a mountain of debt but overcame it. Graham won over the confidence of the reading public and transformed The Star into a major metropolitan newspaper built on improved news coverage and an independent editorial policy.

Graham used The Star to promote the improvement of public health in Montreal, which was in a dangerous state by the 1880s. In 1885, an epidemic of smallpox was imminent. To counter it, widespread vaccination was needed. However, a fanatical charlatan doctor named Joseph-Emery Coderre ran a scare campaign against it. A professor of botany at the Montreal School of Medicine and Surgery and a leading member of Montreal's French medical community, Coderre had been fervently against the vaccine since the 1860s. He had seen many of his patients die as a result of it and was convinced that they were inoculated with smallpox germs instead of medicine, and that the vaccine was used to deliberately spread smallpox and other diseases such as syphilis. Dr. Coderre had been running his anti-vaccination campaign since the 1870s and had gained support from Montreal's poor, working class and French-speaking population, who were mainly based in the city's east end. To counter it, Dr. Coderre introduced his own patent medicine called Sirop des Enfants du Dr. Coderre. Graham believed that Dr. Coderre's anti-vaccination campaign was nonsense and through The Star, tried to stop the doctor's rants with advertisements, articles, and petitions. But Graham was not successful and the smallpox vaccinations were discontinued. As a consequence, smallpox spread across Montreal in epidemic proportions and thousands died.

The Star took action and published articles about the smallpox epidemic, its ravages, and the number of new cases each day. Frustrated by City Hall's continued inaction, Graham and a group of Board of Trade members demanded that City Hall take measures to conquer the epidemic. City aldermen decided to appoint some of the group members to the Board of Health, including Graham, who headed a special committee to see what could be done.

Graham believed that isolating patients was another solution to conquering the smallpox epidemic and helped set up isolation wards, which helped curb the spread of smallpox. The vaccination ban was lifted.

In 1908, Hugh Graham was knighted as Lord Atholstan for his contributions to the British Empire (although Prime Minister Sir Wilfrid Laurier prevented an earlier attempt at knighthood because Graham was a supporter of the rival Conservative Party). Hugh Graham, Lord

**F**or the rest of his life, Graham led the fight for improved health care in Montreal. He launched a campaign for pasteurized milk, was a founder of the Montreal Children's Hospital, organized the Health League to combat tuberculosis and other diseases, and contributed hundreds of thousands of dollars toward its operations. He was also a generous philanthropist, and contributed substantial amounts of money to aid Montreal's disadvantaged citizens.

Atholstan, died in January of 1938 at the age of 89. In an editorial published in *The Montreal Daily Star* on January 28, 1938, the following was written about the impact of Lord Atholstan's death: "The empty place he leaves will be very constantly in the consciousness of the Canadian people for a long time. Philanthropy will have lost its fugleman. Charity will have lost its sure and ever benevolent banker. Public spirit will often pause, waiting for his voice of leadership."

**In 1935, after 10 years of experimenting, Joseph-Armand Bombardier invented the snowmobile, a vehicle that helped rural doctors reach their snowbound patients more quickly. What was the name of the more lightweight snowmobile model introduced in 1959?**

➥**The Ski-Doo.** Born in Valcourt, Quebec, in 1907, Joseph-Armand Bombardier originally studied for the priesthood. However, his passion was for everything and anything mechanical. In 1922, at the age of 15, Bombardier invented the first prototype of what was to be the snowmobile, a four-passenger sleigh frame with an engine and a spinning wooden propeller in the back.

Two years later, Bombardier went to Montreal to apprentice as a mechanic. During that time, he learned the essentials of mechanics. He also taught himself English by reading science and technical journals, all of which were only available in English.

He returned to Valcourt in 1925 and set up his own mechanics business. During the winter months, Bombardier continuously tinkered with his snowmobile, a hobby that lasted 10 years. He also developed the device that formed the nucleus of what would make the snowmobile run: a rubber-encased sprocket interlocked with a traction device encased in rubber. This set-up allowed the necessary shock absorption and propulsion to move a vehicle through the most distasteful of winter conditions.

This tiny sprocket, which was patented in 1937, would form the beginnings of the Bombardier corporation and now serves as its logo.

In 1935, Bombardier's first commercial snowmobile was completed. Called the B7 ("B" for Bombardier, "7" for the number of passengers it would carry), it contained a Ford chassis with skis in front for steering. One year later, a new model of the B7 was introduced with a plywood body on the chassis that resembled the Volkswagen Beetle. Sold at $1,000 per unit, the B7 snowmobile was a success not only with country doctors but also taxi drivers, innkeepers, milkmen, utility workers and funeral directors. By 1939, Bombardier had produced 50 units of the B7.

Understanding the importance of good marketing to increase sales, Bombardier recruited mechanics who could double as sales agents, and had them take the B7 on trips that would show potential customers its abilities. Bombardier himself rode the B7 up the long toboggan slide situated near the Château Frontenac in Quebec City. The Ski-Doo's success was also largely in part due to effective marketing. Throughout the 1960s, the Ski-Doo was used in international snowmobile races and company sponsored expeditions to the Arctic (including a 1966 trip that included CBS News correspondent Charles Kuralt).

After World War II, Bombardier and his snowmobile were experiencing a great deal of success. In 1959, a new lightweight snowmobile was introduced as a replacement for dogsleds, used by fur trappers, gold prospectors, and missionaries. The new snowmobile was to be called the Ski Dog. When a typographical error in the promotional brochure accidentally changed its name to the Ski-Doo, Bombardier decided to stick with this new name, thinking it sounded better than the original.

Between 1959 and 1990, Bombardier became the chief supplier of snowmobiles, with over $183 million in gross sales between 1965 and 1971. Unfortunately, Joseph-Armand Bombardier did not live long enough to enjoy this new level of success with the Ski-Doo. He died of cancer on February 18, 1964, at the age of 56.

However, the Bombardier legacy continues to this day. With the name change to Bombardier Inc. in 1981, the company has branched out to aircraft (including the Challenger and Dash-8), subway trains, and a maritime version of the Ski-Doo called the Sea-Doo.

**What existing bank, known as Canada's first bank, was established in 1817 by Scottish merchant John Richardson, and was modelled after the American banking system?**

→**The Bank of Montreal.** Richardson, who had a vast knowledge of the American banking system, tried to establish the Bank of Montreal as early as 1792. At the time, Montreal was quickly becoming an important centre of commerce and was the hub for exporting crops to England and importing goods from the US.

Inspired by the establishment of the Bank of the United States by Alexander Hamilton the year before, Richardson felt that a bank was needed in Montreal and wanted to base his bank on the American banking system: based on capital and mercantile credit, and which would serve the fiscal, financial, and commercial needs of the city.

Unfortunately, the project fell through. It was felt that the Canadian economy was not sophisticated enough to warrant a bank.

For the following 10 years, things began to change for Montreal as the city became the fastest-growing city in North America, due to its active fur trade industry between Montreal, Vermont, and Upper Canada. Merchants also hoped that Montreal would one day become a major port city.

In 1807, John Richardson hoped to revive the idea of opening a bank in Montreal and, to launch this project, Richardson, who was also a member of the Lower Canada legislature, introduced a bill to incorporate the bank, which passed at first reading. But during and after the War of 1812, three more attempts to establish this bank failed. In January of 1817, Richardson and a group of eight Montreal merchants and legislators decided to take matters into their own hands and open a bank without a charter. On May 29, the Articles of Association of the Montreal Bank were adopted and signed the following month.

On October 23, 1817, the newly formed Bank of Montreal published this notice in several Montreal newspapers: "The bank will begin its operations on Monday, the 3rd of November next. Bank hours from 10 o'clock AM to 3 o'clock PM."

With a capital of $350,000, the Bank of Montreal's first branch was located on St-Paul Street, in the centre of Montreal's business district. It employed seven people in addition to the bank's first president John Gray, who travelled five miles per day to get to his office from his home (which broke the usual custom of merchants living above their businesses).

Two years later, the Bank of Montreal moved to its permanent quarters on St-Jacques Street in Montreal's very first building constructed specifically as a bank, and where they stayed until 1847.

**What controversial Montreal-based French language media magnate built a concert hall near his home in Sainte-Adèle to hear major symphony concerts nearby?**

➡**Pierre Péladeau.** Born in Outremont on April 11, 1925, Péladeau was one of seven children. His father was a successful lumber merchant and his mother was a teacher.

At the age of 13, Péladeau began showing signs of the entrepreneurial spirit that would one day make him a legend. He began selling refreshments at an Outremont tennis club and sold Christmas trees to help pay his tuition and expenses at the University of Montreal, where he earned a master's degree in philosophy, and then at McGill University, where he studied law.

It was while at McGill that Péladeau began his career in the media/ publishing business. With $1,500 borrowed from his mother, Péladeau bought a weekly newspaper called the *Journal de Rosemont*. Realizing the huge business potential of community weekly newspapers, Péladeau then proceeded to buy four more weeklies that served Montreal's French-speaking population.

In 1964, when the powerful French-language daily *La Presse* was in the midst of a seven-month strike, Péladeau took advantage of the situation and launched his flagship newspaper *Le Journal de Montréal*. Using a formula that mixed sex, scandal, sports, and sensationalism, Péladeau turned the paper into the biggest and most profitable French language daily in North America. In the 1970s, to make the paper a bit more respectable, he hired some of Montreal's best French-language journalists, and recruited Parti Québécois leader René Lévesque as a guest columnist after he lost the 1970 provincial election.

From there, Péladeau's media empire snowballed. He beat *People Magazine* by a decade when he launched a string of weeklies such as *Échos Vedettes* that were dedicated to the Quebec celebrity scene, which became very popular and profitable. Today, his Quebecor Inc., a business he launched in 1965, includes four dailies, 42 weeklies (including

*The Winnipeg Sun* and the *Montreal Mirror)*, book and magazine publishing and distribution endeavours, eight Archambeault music stores, pulp and paper mills, multimedia interests, and is Canada's largest commercial printing operation. As of September 30, 1997, it boasted assets of nearly $7.4 billion.

Although known for his keen business and investment acumen, Péladeau's aggressive style of conducting business and his loose tongue mired him in controversy. In 1989, he was accused of male chauvinism when he said that women had no place in business boardrooms because "they seduce too much". He then went on to anger Quebec's English-speaking population when he admitted that he only spoke English when he could make money doing so.

Controversy aside, Péladeau was also a generous philanthropist. He built the Pavillon des Arts in his hometown of Sainte-Adèle, north of Montreal, so he could attend symphony orchestra concerts near his home, because he was a fan of classical and chamber music. He also built the Centre Pierre-Péladeau, a concert hall with superior acoustics, at the Université du Québec à Montréal (UQAM). He supported the training of guide dogs for the visually impaired, was a major benefactor of the Orchestre Métropolitain and in 1996, donated $1 million to a relief fund to aid victims of the Saguenay region floods.

n an interview conducted for Radio-Canada's Réseau de l'Information (RDI) at his Sainte-Adèle home (and not aired until after his death), Péladeau said that he did not want anyone to fuss over him when he died. "I warned my people, I don't want any death notice in the newspaper. Not at all. When I go, I'm gone, I disappear, bye-bye". However, against his wishes, *Le Journal de Montréal* published a 32-page memorial edition about his life and career.

Pierre Péladeau died of heart failure on Christmas Eve of 1997, at the age of 72. Before dying, he requested that his children take charge of different aspects of the Quebecor empire, therefore avoiding messy squabbles over who would take over the family business. Quebecor is currently being run by his son Pierre-Karl Péladeau.

In 1953, Donald Gordon, the controversial president of the Canadian National Railway (CNR), transformed an eyesore lot in the centre of downtown Montreal by building a hotel. What was the name of this famous Montreal hotel?

↪**The Queen Elizabeth Hotel.** In the 1930s, a 24-acre hole in the middle of downtown Montreal was an eyesore for the city's landscape. To fill some of this space, the CNR built the Central Station terminal, which was a squat, low structure on Dorchester Street. But this only covered part of the gaping hole.

In 1952, Canadian National Railway (CNR) president Donald Gordon saw this piece of real estate as having potential for pulling in revenue. The CNR was in good financial standing and believed that, with the number of conventions on the rise in Montreal, the city needed a new hotel. Although this lot was considered ugly, it was above an underground city, near the expanded Central Station terminal, and near the new CNR headquarters. The location was ideal.

Gordon made this venture the CNR's flagship project. At a potential cost of $20 million, he hoped that this new hotel complex would lead to the construction of brand new office buildings, as well as high-class stores and theatres that would not only transform the city, but increase the affluence of the CNR in the business world.

But the major sticking point of this hotel project was its name, which many believed had to reflect Montreal's French-Canadian character, which in turn would attract tourists. Some of the names considered included the Champlain, Maisonneuve, Bonaventure and Voyageur.

*The Queen Elizabeth Hotel in 1965. Some of the names proposed for it included the Maisonneuve, Champlain, Voyageur and Bonaventure.*

By the time the project was unveiled to the press in October of 1953, the hotel was still nameless. The following month, on November 3, 1953, Gordon announced that the new hotel would be named the Queen Elizabeth Hotel.

Gordon's choice angered many. A French-Canadian Member of Parliament introduced a motion in the House of Commons to change the name to Château Maisonneuve, the St. Jean Baptiste Society circulated a petition signed by 250,000 people, and *The Toronto Telegram* criticized Gordon for using a monarch's name for a hotel being run by an American hotel chain (in November of 1954, Gordon had signed a five-year deal with the Hilton hotel chain to run the Queen Elizabeth Hotel).

Ignoring the criticism, Gordon oversaw each aspect of the hotel's construction, from the colour of the bathroom basins to the tableware and drapes. On April 16, 1958, the Queen Elizabeth Hotel officially opened its doors.

A three-day celebration ensued, which included a wide range of festivities such as luncheons, a fashion show, and a charity ball. It also attracted 600 special guests ranging from federal, provincial, and municipal government officials, business leaders, Montreal society figures, and celebrities from the entertainment world. John Fisher, head of the Canadian Tourist Association, was very optimistic about the hotel and its impact on the future of Montreal's economy. He told *The Montreal Star* that the opening festivities alone "has done more to draw attention to Canada's attractions than any other single event".

In the summer of 1958, approximately two months after its opening, the Queen Elizabeth Hotel welcomed its first royal visitor. Princess Margaret, Queen Elizabeth's sister, visited Montreal, and a gala ball was held in her honour at the hotel. Before the ball, she was escorted by mayor Sarto Fournier to a concert featuring music from German composer Johann Sebastian Bach. However, sometime between the concert and the beginning of the ball, the princess mysteriously disappeared, and never showed up for the latter event. According to the late E.J. (Elsie Jean) Gordon, who was *The Gazette*'s society columnist at the time, the princess was rather bored by the all-Bach concert. Mayor Fournier agreed with the princess' dislike of Bach's music, telling Gordon: "I don't go much for this guy Bach."

Within five years, the Queen Elizabeth Hotel established a reputation for itself as one of Montreal's finest and largest hotels, and it retains that reputation to this day. The 21-storey, 1,216-room hotel is still a favourite with tourists, businessmen and organizations. It contains 17 dining rooms and lounges, 11 private salons, five banquet halls and four exhibit areas (its Grand Salon can hold up to 1,000 people at a time). The hotel also contains the Beaver Club, an exclusive restaurant that is an exact replica of a fur traders' club dating back to Montreal's colonial period.

**Which Dublin-born but Montreal-based industrialist was responsible for the formation of the utility that later became Hydro-Quebec, and served on the board of more corporations than any other Canadian businessman?**

**Sir Herbert Holt.** Born in Dublin, Ireland, in 1856, Holt arrived in Canada in 1875 with only $4 in his pocket. He began working with a construction contractor and moved on to help construct a railway in Haliburton, Ontario. His hard work, energy, and self-application allowed Holt to quickly work his way up the ladder and, by the age of 25, he was promoted to superintendent of construction work on the Credit Valley Railroad.

When the Canadian Pacific Railway (CPR) was being expanded west, Holt was put in charge of constructing sections of the CPR in the prairies and British Columbia. He expanded the CPR's lines into Quebec, New Brunswick and Maine, and had the opportunity to witness the historic driving of the last spike of the CPR at Eagle's Pass, British Colombia, in 1885.

Holt settled in Montreal in 1892 and quickly became one of Canada's most prominent business leaders. When he showed interest in the Montreal Gas Company, he was appointed president. He began merging with other local utilities and formed Montreal Light, Heat and Power, which, in the early 1960s, became part of Hydro-Quebec. In 1908, Holt also became the president of the Royal Bank of Canada. Under his leadership, the bank absorbed five other banks and managed to raise the Royal Bank's capital to $35 million and its assets to an astounding $956 million.

Over the course of his life, Holt served on the board of directors of 200 major Canadian corporations, including Sun Life, the Montreal Tramways Commission, Dominion Textile and Holt Renfrew.

Like any major business leader, Holt was known for his generous philanthropy. During World War II, he donated $250,000 to the Wives for

Britain Fund to purchase warplanes for Britain. Holt wrote this note to accompany his contribution: "Enclosed you will find my cheque for $250,000 to buy Spitfires. I am contributing this as a slight recognition of what Lord Beaverbrook [a British newspaper baron born in New Brunswick as Max Aitken] has done for the nation and the flying service."

Sir Herbert Holt died on September 28, 1941, at the age of 85. *The Montreal Daily Star* remembered Holt as a "giant of industry", "a great leader of finance" and "a foremost leader in business".

**Since 1786, the Molson family has been associated with their beer-brewing industry. However, the Molsons have been involved in other ventures, including banking, sports, and the construction of Canada's first steamboat. What was the name of this steamboat?**

↪ *Accommodation.*

In 1782, John Molson arrived in Montreal from England to seek new opportunities for himself. England was going through an agricultural depression and Montreal was flourishing, becoming the nerve centre for the growing fur trade, as well as a strategic supply base for the British Army.

At the time, the preferred beverage of all newly established adventurers and traders was beer. It was deemed safer than tea because it was not made with unsanitary water. Seeing this niche, Molson decided that the times were ideal to establish a brewery. In 1786, with eight bushels of barley and all of his money, Molson launched the Molson's Brewery in a small log cabin located in the rural Montreal district of St. Mary's Current. Six months after the opening, Molson could not keep up with the increasing demand for his beer. He sold 4,000 gallons of it by the end of his first year of business and, within 10 years, was selling 50,000 gallons of ale per year.

By the turn of the 19th century, trade was growing between Montreal and the northeastern United States, through its main artery, the St. Lawrence River. The upcoming construction of the Lachine Canal would also facilitate shipping along the St. Lawrence River.

Molson once again saw an opportunity: the potential of maritime trading. He believed that the solution to negotiating the rapids was to build a boat powered by steam. His interest was heightened when he learned of Robert Fulton's inaugural steamship *Claremont,* launched in 1807, and which started the first commercial steamboat service running from Albany to New York City. One year later, Molson started Canada's first steamboat service.

He hired two British men, John Bruce and John Jackson, both skilled at shipbuilding. While Molson would put up the cost of the shipbuilding, approximately 2,000 pounds, the profits and losses of the boat, once completed, would be shared by all three.

The steamboat *Accommodation* was completed on October 9, 1809, and on November 1, was ready for its maiden voyage from Montreal to Quebec City. However, despite advertising, only 10 of the 20 berths with meals and stowage facilities were booked for the maiden voyage. The fare for the 66-hour journey was $9 from Montreal to Quebec City, and $8 for the return voyage (higher going toward Quebec City because the boat went against the current, hence consuming more fuel and provisions).

During its brief first year of operation, *Accommodation* lost money and continued to lose money in 1810. In 1811, Molson started to dismantle *Accommodation.* According to biographer Karen Molson (a seventh-generation Molson), John Molson carefully removed the boat's cabin and had it converted into a summer cottage for himself.

However, Molson did not abandon the idea of running a steamboat transportation business. His second steamboat, *Swiftsure,* was more powerful, more luxurious, and accommodated more passengers (up to 500 people) — and was profitable. Until the mid-1800s, the Molsons' steamboat operation was profitable and helped improve beer sales along their Montreal-Quebec City route.

The Molson family empire has held diverse business holdings including a bank, a sugar refinery, office supply companies, chemical manufacturers, Vilas Furniture, Beaver Lumber (which was sold to Home Depot in 1998), Molstar Sports and Entertainment, and perhaps its best-known acquisition, the Montreal Canadiens hockey club, which they owned from 1957 to 1972 and from 1978 to 2001. Today, Molson Inc. concentrates solely on the business that patriarch John Molson established in 1786: beer making and distribution. They own and operate seven breweries across Canada and have annual beer sales of over $2 billion.

**What Montreal-based 19th century railway baron saved the Canadian Pacific Railway, became its president, built railroads in Cuba and Guatemala, but was born in the United States?**

→**Sir William Cornelius Van Horne,** a man who lived and worked by the credo "I eat all I can, I drink all I can, I smoke all I can and I don't give a damn for anything," was born in 1843 in Wills County, Illinois.

Van Horne ended his schooling in 1857 at the age of 14. Soon after, he became interested in the railroad industry, particularly in the telegraphing operation. By the age of 15, he became a full-fledged qualified telegraph operator and by 27, was running the telegraph operation for the Chicago and Alton Railroad. Four years later, he became the president of the Southern Minnesota Railroad.

It was during Van Horne's time as general superintendent of the Chicago, Milwaukee and St. Paul Railroad that he first heard about a railway being built in Canada but which was falling on hard times: the Canadian Pacific Railway (CPR). In October of 1881, he was approached by Canadian stock promoter and railroad builder James Jerome Hill to see if he was interested in supervising the construction of the troubled CPR. Van Horne accepted and was hired as the CPR's railway general on November 1, 1881.

Van Horne faced an uphill battle. Rocked by the Pacific Scandal of 1873, in which Prime Minister John A. Macdonald accepted bribes by Montreal businessman Sir Hugh Allan in order to obtain lucrative contracts to build the CPR, and a devastating economic depression during the mid-1870s, the struggling railroad had barely laid 300 miles of track since the start of its construction earlier in 1881. Van Horne pledged that 500 miles of track would be completed by the end of 1882. By that time, over 417 miles of the CPR's main track were in operation.

Over the next three years, the CPR made great strides across the inhospitable Canadian West, yet by 1885, the railroad was operating at a loss and was $400,000 in debt. Prime Minister Macdonald was hesitant to grant it money from the federal government. His main priority was the prevention of a potential rebellion in Saskatchewan, led by Metis leader Louis Riel. Van Horne compromised by offering to transport troops to Saskatchewan via completed sections of the CPR, to help crush the Riel Rebellion. Macdonald accepted and, in July of 1885, the House of Commons passed a bill offering financial aid to the CPR, saving the railroad.

The CPR was completed on November 7, 1885. Three years later, Van Horne was named president of the CPR. From his headquarters at

Windsor Station, Van Horne helped make the railroad into a large-scale integrated transportation network. He built grain elevators along the prairies and constructed prestigious hotels such as the Banff Springs Hotel in Alberta and the Château Frontenac in Quebec City. These hotels were originally intended as meal stop stations for the railroad so that the heavy cumbersome dining cars would not have to travel up the steep, hilly upgrades along the route. As well, Van Horne was constantly improving and upgrading the CPR.

In 1895, Van Horne became the first non-British subject to be knighted and took this new honour with a degree of modesty. When he arrived at his office on the morning that his knighthood was announced, the doorman greeted him as Sir William. Van Horne responded to this new title in his usual manner: "OH HELL!"

Van Horne remained president of the CPR until 1898, when he stepped down. But he became restless and impatient with his retirement and after the Spanish-American War, undertook the rebuilding of Cuba's railroad and became the president of the Cuba Railway Company. The government of the Central American Republic of Guatemala heard about Van Horne's accomplishments in Cuba and asked him to help build their railroad. Under Van Horne's direction, the Trans-Guatemala Railway was completed in 1904 and ran 300 miles from Guatemala City to the republic's Atlantic coast.

ccording to Pierre Berton in his book *The Last Spike*: "[Van Horne's] appetites appeared to be gargantuan. He ate prodigiously and was known as a man who fed his workmen generously. He could sit up all night winning at poker and go to work the following morning without showing a trace of fatigue. He liked his cognac, his whiskey, and his fine French vintages, but he did not tolerate drunkenness in himself or others. Inebriates were fired out of hand. So were slackers, dunces, cravens, cowards, slow-pokes and labour organizers."

Sir William Cornelius Van Horne died on September 11, 1915, at the age of 72. When it was learned that Sir William had died, the CPR system halted its entire operation for five minutes in his memory. The Cuban government called for a national day of mourning. He was buried in Joliet, Illinois.

# MONTREAL
## IN THE SPOTLIGHT

### movies, tv shows and books featuring montreal

**In which Marx Brothers movie is Montreal mentioned during a witty exchange of lines between Groucho and Chico?**

➥*Animal Crackers* (1930). Originally performed by the Marx Brothers on Broadway in 1928–1929, *Animal Crackers* takes place in the Long Island home of socialite Mrs. Rittenhouse (Margaret Dumont), who hosts two major events: the unveiling of a valuable painting she acquired, and a celebration to honour the return to America of the famed African explorer, Captain Jeffrey T. Spaulding (Groucho). Following a scene when Captain Spaulding delivers his famous "one morning I shot an elephant in my pajamas" speech, Emmanuel Ravelli (Chico) plays a tune on the piano, where this dialogue occurs:

GROUCHO: Say if you get near a song, play it.

CHICO: I can't think of the finish.

GROUCHO: That's strange and I can't think of anything else.

CHICO: Know what I think? I think I went past it.

GROUCHO: Well if you come around again, jump off.

CHICO: I once kept this up for three days.

GROUCHO: You wouldn't consider hush money, would you?

CHICO: I can't get it now. I gotta wait for inspiration.

GROUCHO: It's about time. Play that song about Montreal.

CHICO: Montreal?

GROUCHO: "I'm a Dreamer, Montreal".

CHICO: I don't know that.

The Montreal reference originated from Act Two of their 1921 vaude-ville revue *On the Mezzanine,* in which Groucho parodied popular songs of the day. "I'm a Dreamer, Montreal" was a parody of a song called "I'm a Dreamer, Aren't we All".

Montreal also has another connection to the Marx Brothers. In his unabashed memoir *The Marx Brothers Scrapbook* (1973), Groucho claims that while on a vaudeville tour stop in Montreal in 1906 when he was 16 years old (he was appearing with Gus Edwards' Postal Telegraph Boys at the time), he got gonorrhea from a local prostitute. "I was an innocent boy," wrote Groucho. "Then I was sorry. You know what they say. Once you have gonorrhea you never get cured."

Whenever Montreal's comedy legacy is brought up, Groucho's little tryst in its red light district is always mentioned.

## In which classic 1930s Alfred Hitchcock thriller was Montreal mentioned in the movie's pivotal opening scene?

→ *The 39 Steps* (1935). In the first scene, the audience is introduced to Richard Hannay (played by Oscar-winning actor Robert Donat), a Canadian vacationing in England. During a stop at an English music hall, he sees a performer called Mr. Memory, a man skilful enough to answer any general knowledge question asked by audience members without the aid of books or resources. Hannay steps up and asks Mr. Memory if he knows the distance between Winnipeg and Montreal. Mr. Memory answers correctly by saying 2,394 kilometres (1,496 miles).

During this same show, a man is murdered in the music hall. After-wards, Hannay harbours a young girl who confesses that she committed the murder, and who says that she is involved with a spy organization called The 39 Steps, which has a top-level military secret that it is ready to sell to a foreign power. That morning, the young girl is found mur-dered in Hannay's hotel room, and Hannay is thrust into a four-day chase from London to Scotland.

*The 39 Steps* was based on a novel by John Buchan, who served as Governor General of Canada from 1935 to 1940. A career writer, historian, lawyer and government official, Buchan published over 90 books in his lifetime, including volumes of biography, history, novels and short fiction. However, it was *The 39 Steps* that became his best-known and most enduring book. He wrote it in 1914 while bedridden, as he recovered from a gastric ailment. He saw the novel as a story that "might amuse the soldiers". When it was published one year later, it became a best-seller and was instrumental in developing the spy novel genre, which included such elements as the extended chase (or "hurried journey"), maniacal or methodical villains who try to push the civilized world to the edge of disaster, and the hero who saves the day through a combination of perseverance, coincidence, and luck.

On February 6, 1940, John Buchan, who as Baron Tweedsmuir of Elsfield served as Canada's Governor General, fell and suffered a concussion following the blockage of a small artery in his brain (known as a thrombosis). Three days later, he was taken from his vice-regal residence of Rideau Hall in Ottawa to the Montreal Neurological Institute, where he underwent two operations to relieve pressure on his brain. He died at the Institute on the evening of February 11 from a pulmonary embolism at the age of 65, just months before he was to finish his term as Governor General of Canada.

Hitchcock had originally wanted to make a film adaptation of Buchan's novel *Greenmantle,* which was based on the life of legendary World War I British army officer Colonel T.E. Lawrence, better known as Lawrence of Arabia. Instead, he chose *The 39 Steps* because, as he told French filmmaker François Truffaut, he was attracted to Buchan's "understatement of highly dramatic ideas".

## What cult classic 1958 science fiction movie took place in Montreal and starred Vincent Price and David (Al) Hedison?

➥ *The Fly.* Hedison played André, a Montreal-based scientist who developed a way of electronically disintegrating objects, and then materializing them at another distant location. However, when he decided to use himself as a guinea pig for an electronic disintegration experiment, a common housefly got in the way. The result: André and the fly switched heads.

Written by future best-selling novelist James Clavell, *The Fly* was set in Montreal but was filmed at the Twentieth Century Fox Studios in Hollywood. Hence, the movie contained no footage of Montreal and the only indications of the film's setting were the French-Canadian names given to the characters, a French-language sign displayed outside a factory, and Montreal-labelled police vehicles.

When *The Fly* played at the Princess Theatre in downtown Montreal in 1958, newspaper advertisements offered $100 to the first person who could prove that the molecular electronic disintegration experiments done in the movie could not happen in real life. Also, a strict rule was enforced that no person could be admitted to the theatre by themselves unless they signed a waiver. The reason behind such an unusual measure was never explained by the theatre's management.

Jacob Siskind, *The Montreal Star's* entertainment critic, praised *The Fly* for its fine acting, effective use of cinematography, and believable fantasy plot. However, Siskind noted one factual inaccuracy with its Montreal setting, in which "the research staff for Twentieth Century Fox boggled when they let Vincent Price offer to take six-year-old Charles Herbert to a film. That sort of thing just doesn't happen in these parts." At the time, a provincial law strictly prohibited that children under the age of 16 be admitted to movie theatres.

*The Fly* is regarded as a cult classic in the science fiction genre and led to two unsuccessful sequels: *Return of the Fly* (1959) and *Curse of the Fly* (1965), and was remade in 1986 by Canadian director David Cronenberg.

**In an episode of *The Simpsons,* Marge offered a brand of gourmet coffee to her guests. This coffee was named after Montreal. What was it called?**

➥**Montreal Morning.** In the episode "Homer vs. Patty and Selma" (which first aired in February of 1995), Homer foolishly lost his life savings when he invested in the pumpkin business but failed to sell his stock before Halloween. With nowhere else to turn, he asked his loathsome, chain-smoking sisters-in-law Patty and Selma for the money needed to get himself out of debt. With the money came their promise not to tell Marge about his financial debacle, but in exchange, Homer virtually became their slave.

Patty and Selma quickly took advantage of the situation and invited themselves over for dinner at his house. With dessert, Marge offered everyone some gourmet Montreal Morning coffee. However, she returned to tell them that she was out of Montreal Morning and only had Nescafé to offer.

Dissatisfied, Patty and Selma revealed Homer's financial secret to Marge. Homer, in a fit of anger, threw the two hated sisters-in-law out of his house . . . literally.

Don't try to find Montreal Morning at your local supermarket . . . that particular brand of coffee never existed (except in Springfield).

**Based on the critically acclaimed stage play by John Pielmeier, what 1985 movie starring Jane Fonda, Anne Bancroft, and Meg Tilly dealt with a murder investigation at a convent outside of Montreal?**

➥*Agnes of God.* Directed by Canadian Norman Jewison (who also directed *Fiddler on the Roof* and *A Soldier's Story*), *Agnes of God* told the story of Dr. Martha Livingston (Fonda), a chain-smoking psychiatrist sent to Montreal to investigate the case of a young Catholic nun, Sister Agnes (Tilly), who mysteriously gave birth to a baby later found strangled to death. Bancroft played the convent's Mother Superior, whose involvement in the case was revealed to be much deeper than suspected.

Filmed on location in an abandoned orphanage on Côte de Liesse Road in Montreal, *Agnes of God* featured several prominent French-Canadian actors including Gabriel Arcand *(The Plouffe Family)* who played a Catholic Monsignor, and veteran Montreal actor/playwright Gratien Gélinas, as Father Martineau, an aging priest.

The movie received mixed reviews. *The New York Times* called it "unsurprising" and "awkward". However, Fonda, Tilly, and Bancroft received much praise for their performances. Tilly went on to win a Golden Globe Award for her role as the mystical Sister Agnes, and was also nominated for an Oscar, along with Bancroft.

"On the screen, 'Agnes of God' now has a great many subsidiary players, several of them cows; the convent is situated outside Montreal, and Mr. Jewison even includes a few barnyard scenes for the sake of atmosphere. There are also ice-skating nuns, who are seen to bear a cute resemblance to penguins, and fleeting glimpses of various convent rituals."
— *The New York Times*, regarding *Agnes of God*'s Montreal location shots

For over 40 years, Mordecai Richler was renowned worldwide as the predominant literary voice of Montreal's Jewish community, a reputation that came with the success of his fourth novel *The Apprenticeship of Duddy Kravitz* (1959). Which Richler novel first featured Montreal's Jewish neighbourhood?

➥*Son of a Smaller Hero* (1955). The book, Richler's second, recounted the story of Noah Adler, the son of a scrap dealer who tried to break away from the confines of Montreal's Jewish ghetto and enter the much closed-off world of the "goyim" (Yiddish for non-Jewish people) during the early 1950s.

Born in 1931, Richler grew up on St-Urbain Street in the heart of Montreal's Jewish community. His father, like Noah Adler's, ran a scrapyard. But Richler rejected his strict religious upbringing at the age of 13, after deciding that he did not agree with his ultra-orthodox grand-father, who continuously beat him with a leather belt for even the most minor of religious infractions. As a consequence, he became a self-confessed atheist.

In 1951, after a short stint studying English at Sir George Williams University (which became part of Concordia University in 1974), Richler left Montreal and toured Spain and Paris. He settled in London in 1954 and, that same year, published his first novel *The Acrobats,* which told the story of a group of disillusioned expatriates living in Spain. Published in Britain and the United States, *The Acrobats* got mixed reviews and was a commercial failure.

For his second novel, Richler turned to his own childhood world, the Main, for his book's setting. According to author William Weintraub in his

*The late Mordecai Richler (centre) on the Fairmount Street set of* Joshua Then and Now *(1984).*

2001 memoir *Getting Started* about his early writing career and friendship with Richler in the 1950s, *Son of a Smaller Hero* was rejected by Putnam, Richler's American publisher, because of the lack of success of *The Acrobats*. However, Walter Allen, a British critic who was also a reader for the English publisher Andre Deutsch, enthusiastically recommended *Son of a Smaller Hero* for publication after reading the manuscript, saying "Richler is the first Canadian who is also a novelist. His book exists on many levels. The city (Montreal) comes through brilliantly . . ."

When the book was finally published in 1955, critics from his hometown were less than kind in their assessment of the book. *The Congress Bulletin,* the Canadian Jewish Congress newspaper, condemned it as a piece of "self-hate" literature and compared it to the vehemently anti-Semitic Nazi newspaper *Der Stürmer.* However, critics abroad had nothing but praise to offer. *The London Times Literary Supplement* wrote that "Mr. Richler's admirable novel recreates the teeming streets, the frustrated passions, the furious inbred life of Montreal's Jewish quarter."

By the time *Duddy Kravitz* was published in 1959, Richler was nominated for a Governor General's Award but lost to *The Watch That Ends The Night* by Montreal-based novelist Hugh MacLennan.

**Which American mystery/thriller writer (known by his single-name pseudonym), used the seedy side of St. Lawrence Boulevard as the setting for his 1976 best-selling murder mystery *The Main?***

➥**Trevanian.** *The Main* dealt with a brutal murder that occurred on St. Lawrence Boulevard, an area portrayed as a grimy slum district inhabited by hookers, pimps, criminals, and numerous different ethnic groups. Investigating the murder is Claude LaPointe, a hard-boiled, bullying, middle-aged ailing Montreal police lieutenant who used his own brand of enforcing the law to bring the case to its rightful conclusion.

St. Lawrence Boulevard's reputation goes back to 1792, when it became the dividing line between Montreal's east and west sectors. In the 1830s, Montreal's principal street became known to its citizens as "St. Laurent du Main" or "St. Lawrence Main" and became a haven for small shops, taverns, artisans, and skilled workers.

It was immediately after World War I that the Main got the multicultural character for which it is known today, after many East European immigrants established their homes and businesses on this main artery. From the 1920s to the 1950s, the Main became the nerve center of Montreal's open city as American bootleggers set up clubs and theatres along the street, which led to violence, commercialized vice and corruption among members of Montreal's police force.

With the election of Jean Drapeau as mayor in 1954, the Main became part of a corruption clean-up campaign. Blocks of buildings were demolished on the lower Main to make way for the construction of new buildings and a new expressway. By the time Trevanian's novel was published in 1976, the Main was about to undergo a transformation from a slum area to a neighbourhood filled with trendy cafes, restaurants, clubs, clothing boutiques, and art galleries.

Trevanian is the pen name of Rodney Whitaker, a former film and drama teacher at the University of Texas in Austin, who also wrote novels under the pseudonyms Nicholas Seare, Benat le Cagat and J.L. Moran. Although an American by birth, in a review of *The Main* published in *The New Yorker,* it was alleged that Trevanian was Canadian.

*The Main* became a best-seller and received positive reviews for its honest yet grim portrayal of St. Lawrence Boulevard's seedy side. In a review published in *Harper's Magazine,* author Evan Connell praised *The Main* for its warm narrative style, its "raffish characters sketched with considerable insight" and Trevanian's feelings for "the moments, the hours, and the seasons of human life."

**What is the name of Brian Moore's award-winning 1960 novel based on Moore's own experiences as a Montreal immigrant, and his years working at *The Gazette* during the late 1940s and early 1950s?**

➥ *The Luck of Ginger Coffey.* Moore arrived in Canada from his native Ireland in 1948. After a year of unsuccessfully looking for work in the newspaper field in Toronto, Moore left for Montreal. He was immediately fascinated by the city's mixture of North American and French cultures. But what especially fascinated Moore was Montreal's seamy underbelly such as the Main area of St. Lawrence Boulevard, where he feasted on tourtière meat pies, French fries and steamed hot dogs, and frequented the numerous bars and erotic shows that peppered the neighbourhood.

Moore called St. Lawrence Boulevard the skid row of Montreal, and admitted that it was the "most fascinating street in Montreal — and no other street compares with it or has anything like its color and variety."

That same year, Moore got a job as a proofreader at *The Gazette* for $30 a week. But editor Harry Larkin recognized Moore's talent and promoted him to reporter. He quickly proved himself to be one of *The Gazette's* most versatile reporters. He also developed his skills as a literary storyteller with a penchant for detail.

An account of Brian Moore's routine as a beat reporter for *The Gazette* during the early 1950s (according to a former colleague at the paper): "He was enterprising, accurate, and — above all — fast. He'd come into the office from an assignment at high speed and seemed to start typing while still in the process of sitting down at his desk. He'd have his story finished while the rest of us were still staring blankly at that old Underwood (typewriter), and adding more sugar to our coffee."

As a sideline to his work at *The Gazette,* Moore wrote a series of paperback thrillers under the pen name of Michael Bryan. One of them, *Intent To Kill,* was a medical thriller that took place at the Montreal Neurological Institute where incidentally, Moore had spent time recovering from brain damage sustained in a boating accident in 1953.

In 1955, Moore published *Judith Hearne,* his first novel under his own name. It was a commercial and critical success. Four years later, Moore wrote his third novel set in Montreal, *The Luck of Ginger Coffey.* The title character, like Moore, was an Irish immigrant in his late 30s who came to Montreal for a better life. Full of hope and ambition, Coffey hit roadblocks and setbacks and ended up with a low-paying job as a newspaper proofreader. The novel offered a vivid portrait of Montreal during the 1950s, at its most inhospitable, dreary time of the year, the winter.

*The Luck of Ginger Coffey* got rave reviews and was a best-seller in the United States, Canada, and in England. Hailed by author Jack Ludwig as "probably the finest novel Canada has seen" *The Luck of Ginger Coffey* won the Governor General's Award for Fiction in 1961, a Canada Council Fellowship, and a Guggenheim Fellowship. The CBC produced a televised version of the book in the summer of 1961, and a feature film based on the book was released in 1964. Filmed on location in Ottawa and Montreal, it starred British actor Robert Shaw (*Jaws* and *The Sting*).

# What is the 1944 best-selling novel that recounts the story of the forbidden love affair between a Jewish soldier from Ontario and a non-Jewish girl from Westmount?

→ *Earth and High Heaven,* by Gwethalyn Graham. Born in Toronto, Graham lived in Montreal for the majority of her life and succeeded in describing life in Montreal during the 1940s, when prejudice was prevalent and lines between classes were clearly drawn.

"Hampered by racial-religious distinctions to start with, relations between the French, English and Jews of Montreal are still further complicated by the fact that all three minority groups suffer from an inferiority complex — the French because they are a minority in Canada, the English because they are a minority in Quebec, and the Jews because they are a minority everywhere."
— *Earth and High Heaven* (1944)

Graham's 1944 novel *Earth and High Heaven* dealt with those exact topics. It told the story of Marc Reiser, a Jewish lawyer from a small town in Ontario who was a soldier in the Canadian Army and was preparing to go overseas to fight in World War II. Marc fell in love with Erica Drake, a non-Jewish Westmount girl and daughter of a wealthy importer. As they announced their marriage, the tensions related to inter-religious relationships surfaced.

The book gained widespread acclaim for its flair for dialogue, its realistic character sketches, its absorbing and mature narrative, and its vivid portrayal of life in Montreal in the early 1940s. *The New York Times* said *Earth and High Heaven* ". . . immerses you in the social life of Montreal — which isn't very different, after all, from the society of any of the older cities of our eastern seaboard. The novel is adult and sophisticated without being glittery." It became a best-seller in North America.

**What is the name of Gabrielle Roy's 1945 novel that tells the story of the Lacasse family and their struggle to survive in the slums of Montreal's St-Henri district during the early years of World War II?**

➥ *The Tin Flute* or *Bonheur d'occasion.* Set in the southern Montreal working class district of St-Henri around 1940, *The Tin Flute* centres around the Lacasse family. The father, Azarius, is an unemployed carpenter; the mother, Rose-Anna, struggles to care for her large brood of children; and Florentine, the eldest daughter, works as a waitress for a dime store's lunch counter, while hoping and trying to find a way out of the hardship and grim poverty of St-Henri.

Author Gabrielle Roy was born in 1909 in St. Boniface, Manitoba, where she worked as a teacher during the 1920s and 1930s. In 1941, she moved to Montreal where she worked as a freelance journalist for various French-language publications such as *Le Bulletin des agriculteurs* (a farming journal), *Le Jour* and *Le Canada.* Living frugally in an apartment on Dorchester Boulevard in the Westmount district, Roy spent her evenings exploring the streets of this elite district. During one of those long walks, Roy accidentally stumbled upon St-Henri and was immediately captivated by the hard life its inhabitants endured.

Roy began to report on the plight of the people of St-Henri in a series of articles for *Le Bulletin des agriculteurs.* They became the basis for her first novel *The Tin Flute,* published in French in 1945. "I had never seen such poverty as there was in St. Henri," Roy admitted in an interview conducted in 1976. "And I never thought what I started writing would grow into a novel. But little by little it did, as the bitter thought came to me that the war was a kind of salvation for so many people living there."

*A 1960s paperback edition of* The Tin Flute, *with Gabrielle Roy's portrait adorning the cover.*

After a slow start due to financial problems, *The Tin Flute* took off when it was published in English in 1947. It garnered widespread acclaim with Canadian and American critics (the *New York Herald Tribune* called it "readable and recommendable"), was chosen as a selection by an American book club, was translated into eight languages, and sold over a million copies around the world. That same year, the novel won both France's prestigious Prix Femina (making Roy the first Canadian author to receive the award) and the Governor General's Award for Fiction, and made Gabrielle Roy the "grande dame" of Canadian literature.

Roy spent the remainder of her life in Quebec City, wrote nine more novels, a short story collection and a volume of memoirs, and won three more Governor General's Awards. She died on July 13, 1984, of a heart attack at the age of 74, just as the film version of *The Tin Flute* was making its world premiere at the Moscow Film Festival. The movie was also chosen as the closing film of the 1984 Montreal World Film Festival.

# BIBLIOGRAPHY

## Books

Ackroyd, Peter. *Dickens*. London: Sinclair-Stevenson Limited, 1990.

Atherton, William Henry. *Montreal 1535–1914, Volume II: Montreal Under British Rule 1760–1914*. Montreal: S.J. Clarke Publishing Company, 1914.

Beatles, The. *The Beatles Anthology*. San Francisco: Chronicle Books, 2000.

Benedict, Michael (Editor). *Canada in the Fifties: From the Archives of Maclean's*. Toronto: Viking, 1999.

Berton, Pierre. *The Last Spike: The Great Railway 1881–1885*. Toronto: McClelland & Stewart, 1971.

Best, Dave. *Canada: Our Century in Sport: 1900–2000*. Markham, Ontario: Fitzhenry & Whiteside, 2001.

Bliss, Michael. *Plague: A Story of Smallpox in Montreal*. Toronto: HarperCollins, 1991.

Bronfman, Saidye. *My Sam: A Memoir By His Wife*. Privately printed, 1982.

Brown, William. *Baseball's Fabulous Montreal Royals*. Montreal: Robert Davies Publishing, 1996.

Charbonneau, Jean-Pierre. *The Canadian Connection*. Montreal: Optimum Publishing Company Limited, 1976.

Choko, Marc H. *The Major Squares of Montreal*. Montreal: Meridian Press, 1990.

Collard, Edgar Andrew. *Montreal Yesterdays*. Toronto: Longmans Canada Limited, 1962.

Collard, Edgar Andrew. *Montreal: The Days That Are No More*. Toronto: Doubleday Canada, 1976.

Collard, Edgar Andrew. *All Our Yesterdays*. Montreal: *The Gazette,* 1988.

Collard, Edgar Andrew. *Montreal Yesterdays: More Stories from All Our Yesterdays*. Montreal: *The Gazette,* 1989.

Comeau, Robert, Luc Desrochers, and Claude V. Marsolais. *Histoire des Maires de Montréal*. Montreal: VLB Éditeur, 1993.

Consentino, Frank. *Canadian Football: The Grey Cup Years*. Toronto: Musson, 1969.

Consentino, Frank, and Glynn Leyshon. *Olympic Gold: Canadian Winners of the Summer Games*. Toronto: Holt, Rinehart & Winston of Canada Limited, 1975.

Demchinsky, Bryan, and Elaine Kalman Naves. *Storied Streets: Montreal in the Literary Imagination*. Toronto: Macfarlane, Walter & Ross, 2000.

Dennison, Merrill. *Canada's First Bank: A History of the Bank of Montreal, Volume 1*. Toronto: McClelland & Stewart, 1967.

Diagram Group, The. *The Rule Book*. New York: St. Martin's Press, 1983.

Diamond, Dan. *Years of Glory 1942–1967: The National Hockey League's Official Book of the Six-Team Era*. Toronto: McClelland & Stewart, 1994.

Dollier de Casson, François. *A History of Montreal 1640–1672*. New York: E.P. Dutton, 1928.

Dow, Leslie Smith. *Anna Leonowens: A Life Beyond the King and I*. Lawrencetown Beach, Nova Scotia: Pottersfield Press, 1991.

Duhamel, Jerome (Editor). *Le Mémorial du Québec*. Montreal: Les Éditions du Mémorial (Québec) Inc., 1979.

Edwards, Peter. *Blood Brothers: How Canada's Most Powerful Mafia Family Runs Its Business*. Toronto: Key Porter Books, 1990.

*Encyclopedia Canadiana, Volume 3*. Toronto: Grolier of Canada, 1970.

Fournier, Louis. *F.L.Q.: The Anatomy of An Underground Movement*. Toronto: NC Press Limited, 1984.

Gibbon, John Murray. *Our Old Montreal*. Toronto: McClelland & Stewart, 1947.

Gilmore, John. *Swinging in Paradise: The Story of Jazz in Montreal*. Montreal: Véhicule Press, 1988.

Gordon, E.J. *E.J. Looking Back*. Montreal: Price Patterson Ltd., 1993.

Gubbay, Aline. *A Street Called The Main: The Story of Montreal's Boulevard Saint-Laurent*. Montreal: Meridian Press, 1989.

Hadekel, Peter, and Ann Gibbon. *Steinberg: The Breakup of A Family Empire*. Toronto: Macmillan of Canada, 1990.

Heymann, C. David. *Liz: An Intimate Biography of Elizabeth Taylor*. Secaucus, New Jersey: Birch Lane Press, 1995.

Irvin, Dick. *Now Back To You, Dick: Two Lifetimes in Hockey*. Toronto: McClelland & Stewart, 1988.

Irvin, Dick. *The Habs: An Oral History of the Montreal Canadiens, 1940–1980*. Toronto: McClelland & Stewart, 1991.

Jasmin, Yves (Editor). *100 Ans d'Actualités 1900–2000*. Montreal: *La Presse*, 1999.

Jenkins, Kathleen. *Montreal: Island City of the St. Lawrence*. Garden City, New York: Doubleday, 1966.

Johnson, Kirk, and David Widgington. *Montreal Up Close: A Pedestrian's Guide to the City*. Montreal: Cumulus Press, 1998.

Kelley, Kitty. *Elizabeth Taylor: The Last Star*. New York: Simon & Schuster, 1981.

Kendall, Brian. *Our Hearts Went Boom: The Beatles' Invasion of Canada*. Toronto: Viking, 1997.

King, Joe. *From the Ghetto to the Main: The Story of the Jews of Montreal*. Montreal: The Montreal Jewish Publication Society, 2000.

Labrèche-Larouche, Michelle. *Emma Albani: International Star*. Montreal: XYZ Publishing, 2001.

Lamb, W. Kaye. *History of the Canadian Pacific Railway*. New York: Macmillan, 1977.

Lanctot, Gustave. *Montreal Under Maisonneuve 1642–1665*. Toronto: Clarke, Irwin & Company, 1969.

Lanken, Dane. *Montreal Movie Palaces: Great Theatres of the Golden Era 1884–1938*. Waterloo, Ontario: Penumbra Press, 1993.

Lazar, Barry. *Tea with Mr. George and Other Adventures in Montreal*. Montreal: Silver Living, 1997.

Leacock, Stephen. *Charles Dickens: His Life and Work*. Garden City, New York: Doubleday Doran & Company, 1934.

Leacock, Stephen. *Montreal: Seaport and City*. Garden City, New York: Doubleday Doran & Company, 1942.

Lewisohn, Mark. *The Complete Beatles Chronicle*. New York: Harmony Books, 1992.

MacDonald, Larry. *The Bombardier Story: Planes, Trains and Snowmobiles*. Toronto: John Wiley & Sons, 2001.

Marelli, Nancy. *Montreal Photo Album: Photographs from the Montreal Archives*. Montreal: Véhicule Press, 1993.

Marrus, Michael R. *Mr. Sam: The Life and Times of Samuel Bronfman*. Toronto: Viking, 1991.

Marsh, James H. (Editor in Chief). *The Canadian Encyclopedia, Year 2000 Edition*. Toronto: McClelland & Stewart, 1999.

Marx, Groucho, and Richard J. Anobile. *The Marx Bros. Scrapbook*. New York: Darien House, 1973.

McKenna, Brian, and Susan Purcell. *Drapeau*. Toronto: Clarke, Irwin & Company Limited, 1980.

McNeil, Bill, and Morris Wolfe. *Signing On: The Birth of Radio in Canada*. Toronto: Doubleday Canada, 1982.

Molson, Karen. *The Molsons: Their Lives and Times 1780–2000*. Willowdale, Ontario: Firefly Books, 2001.

Montreal Society of Architecture. *Explaining Montreal*. Montreal: Gregy De Pencier Publications, 1974.

Mouton, Claude. *The Montreal Canadiens: An Illustrated History of A Hockey Dynasty*. Toronto: Key Porter Books, 1987.

Nash, Jay Robert. *The Encyclopedia of World Crime*. Wilmette, Illinois: Crimebooks, Inc., 1990.

Newman, Peter C. *Flame of Power: The Story of Canada's Greatest Businessmen*. Toronto: McClelland & Stewart, 1965.

Newman, Peter C. *Bronfman Dynasty: The Rothschilds of the New World*. Toronto: McClelland & Stewart, 1978.

Percival, W.P. *The Lure of Montreal*. Toronto: The Ryerson Press, 1964.

Prevost, Robert. *Montreal: A History*. Toronto: McClelland & Stewart, 1993.

Radwanski, George. *Trudeau*. Toronto: Macmillan of Canada, 1978.

Rampersad, Arnold. *Jackie Robinson: A Biography*. New York: Alfred A. Knopf, 1997.

Roberts, Leslie. *Montreal: From Mission Colony to World City*. Toronto: Macmillan of Canada, 1969.

Robinson, Jackie. *I Never Had It Made*. New York: Putnam, 1972.

Sampson, Denis. *Brian Moore: The Chameleon Novelist*. Toronto: Doubleday Canada, 1998.

Saywell, John. *Canadian Annual Review*. Toronto: University of Toronto Press, 1963, 1964.

Schull, Joseph. *Rebellion: The Rising in French Canada 1837*. Toronto: Macmillan of Canada, 1971.

Schull, Joseph. *The Great Scot: A Biography of Donald Gordon*. Montreal: McGill-Queen's University Press, 1979.

Stewart, Sandy. *From Coast to Coast*. Toronto: CBC Enterprises, 1985.

Waller, Adrian. *No Ordinary Hotel: The Ritz-Carlton's First Seventy-Five Years*. Montreal: Véhicule Press, 1989.

Weintraub, William. *City Unique: Montreal Days and Nights in the 1940s and '50s*. Toronto: McClelland & Stewart, 1996.

Weintraub, William. *Getting Started: A Memoir of the 1950s*. Toronto: McClelland & Stewart, 2001

Wolf, Joshua, and Cecile Grenier. *Discover Montreal*. Montreal: Libre Expression, 1993.

Woods, Jr., Shirley E. *The Molson Saga 1763–1983*. Toronto: Doubleday Canada, 1983.

## Magazine articles

Burke, Tim. "Manhunt!" *Maclean's* (June 1, 1963).

Clark, Gerald. "TV Comes to Canada and C.B.C. hopes it'll be better than in the U.S.". *Weekend Picture Magazine* (September 6, 1952).

Clarke, Wayne. "Welcome To Paradise". *Weekend* (February 7, 1976).

Davis, Paul McKenna. "Big Stuff with the Small Fry". *The Montreal Star* (June 22, 1968).

Gray, John. "Our First Century — A Lot of It Was Fun". *The Montreal Star: One Hundred Years of Growth, Turmoil and Change* (January 16, 1969).

Stall, Robert. "Jagger: 'Rock 'n' Roll Is Violent Music, Man'". *Weekend* (September 2, 1972).

## Newspapers

Microfilm archives from *The Montreal Star* (1873–1979) and *The Montreal Gazette* (1868–present).

# INDEX

Page numbers in italic indicate a picture or boxed text. Where a page number appears in both italic and regular font, it indicates a photograph or drawing of the person or place named.

## Photo credits

Front cover (Montreal skyline from Mount Royal): © *CORBIS/MAGMA*

Page 12, 44 (tray), 156: Andrew Gryn Collection

Page 16, 59, 117, 123: McGill University Archives

Page 19: *The Montreal Star,* July 18, 1972

Page 22: Andy Nulman Collection

Page 31: *The Montreal Star,* March 5, 1965

Page 33, 90: Stuart Nulman

Page 44 (guidebook), 85, 135, 161: Stuart Nulman Collection

Page 48, 118: Graham MacDonald Collection

Page 60, 62, 69, 97, 99, 143: Ville de Montréal, Gestion de documents et archives

Page 65: *The Montreal Star,* October 26, 1957

Page 83: Archives *La Presse*

Page 107: *The Montreal Gazette,* November 1, 1949

Page 110: Joe Morena

Page 119: *The Montreal Daily Star,* May 7, 1910

Page 176: Andrew Gryn

# ABOUT THE AUTHOR

The definition of Stuart Nulman is, in a nutshell, a harvester of information. Born in the 60s, raised by mogul parents of the fashion industry — smack in the middle of Montreal's heyday — Stuart had it all. Though a hockey star he would never be, movies, music and books were the nurturers of his youth.

Armed with a Concordia University degree, Nulman quickly made his mark on the media world. From Radio Canada International, where he trained, to notoriety as a local columnist/reviewer, to the foundation of research that he helped create for the Just for Laughs museum, to regular appearances as a film and book expert on Montreal's top talk radio station CJAD, well, on and on it goes.

When opportunity landed Stuart with the chance to write about one of his favourite topics, Montreal, destiny had its match. Microfilm that hadn't seen the light of day was uncovered, and two years later, voila. Favourite memory: discovering his parents' engagement announcement. Favourite wish: to have been old enough to appreciate Expo 67. Hope for the future: to have his next About the Author read "Stuart Nulman, best-selling author, lives with his wife and three kids in Montreal, New York and Florida."

Your contributions for a second volume of *Beyond the Mountain* are welcome. If you have any interesting stories or anecdotes about Montreal's past, log on to the Callawind Publications website at www.callawind.com to share them with Stuart.